WITHOUT PREJUDICE

ALL THE CHARACTERS IN THIS BOOK ARE Fictitious ANY RESEMBLANCE TO ANY ACTUAL PERSON LIVING OR DEAD IS PURELY COINCIDENTAL.

ALTHOUGH YOU MAY OBSERVE SIMILARITIES WITH SOME OF THE REAL LIFE CROOKS AND ABUSERS THAT EXIST IN THE CYBER WORLD

LETS FACE IT HERE ARE MANY.

To the illegal scammer's felons and pure bad people that cruise the inter-net.

SHAME ON YOU

SHIT HAPPENS

IT IS THE WAY OF THE WORLD!

I dedicate this book to my family and friends.

There has been a lot of fun and laughter with the friends I have met on the internet.

I managed to contact some very nice people through

Marcus Friends site

www.plentyoffish.com

His site is very safe and supports the site members if there is a hint of a scammer or abuser.

Other sites I actually joined were fun! Some I joined were just continuous payment and a name on a database! Some sites were free for women! There are so many to chose from and the fact that some are affiliated to other sites so your information is shared or sold go on Have fun.But remember only to give out information you chose to give. Take care!

www.match.com

www.mate1.com

www.perfectmatch.com

www.datingdirect.com

www.true.com

www.loopylove.com

www.sugardaddie.com

www.millionaire.com

www.craigslist.com

www.eharmony.com

www.tagged.com

CEI

CHIP

ED

DISCRETO

DAVID

DONALD

DURSUN

FIGO

FRED

GINO

HARRY

JOHN W

JIMMY G

MIKE

PASCUAL

SECRET SMILE

Tiff

Louis-James

WOLFGANG

Janice

Janet

Heather

Karin

Raelyn

Love Crosses the Pond.com

Author

Pauline Smart

Publisher www.lulu.com/paulinesmart

Editor

Pauline Smart

INTERNET DATING?

As Singletons we are all searching for that!

"Special Someone"

The bedtime stories our parents read to us as little children prepared us to live in a fairytale world.

"For a young Princess the promise of."

"One Day our Prince would come". Was a story we enacted throughout our childhood years! And oh how we as grown ladies know we have to kiss a few frogs now and then? Sometimes our budding prince becomes the beast in our lives!

We pick ourselves up! Dust our selves down, lock ourselves in our Ivory tower put a teat on a bottle of wine. Have a good cry then bravely exit to surf the internet dating from our safe haven we step a little closer to another Prince charming or is it a cyber make believe world?

The Internet offers a dating system, which allows individuals to meet online and possibly develop a social, romantic or sexual relationship.

Then there is NET DATING SERVICES!

These provide un-moderated matchmaking! Through the use of personal computers and the internet. Chat rooms replace bar rooms. You sometimes get a raised eyebrow from family members. Hey isn't that Internet dating dangerous?

YES IT IS!

So is drinking in a bar! You can get your drink spiked!

Meet a man and he is out sans wife!

Unfortunately there are dangers and horror stories concerning Internet dating for both men and women!

Mail order "Russian and Ukrainian Brides" for men.

Go visit these countries and you see some odd looking couples that under normal circumstances the couples would never engage in a date. Money talks. Then lady walks! Free in hopefully for the Russian or Ukraine woman in the U.S.A./UK. How many men have lost their hearts or wallets to the scam?

Desperado's for UK or USA residence

Fraudulent Dating Agencies!

Match.com and Yahoo Personals have infect been taken to court.

I had the misfortune to be enticed onto match.com and found my self E-mailing a computer-generated robot that was a perfect match for me?

The use of Russian and Nigerian scammers that post professional photo shoot images to entice you onto their site, at a sign up fee for you!

Be extremely careful. These guys are looking for your personal information, the laws in their country. None…

There is no law against cyber crime in Nigeria or Russia!

The countries are corrupt!

Once they have your details monetary wise and personal data you will have no just cause to retrieve anything you have taken from you!

Be careful!

Check out other scam agencies! The same images are on those sites? You will be enticed to E-mail them to your personal E-mail address! Then they hook you for money, usually paid through Western Union. Before you know it you are paying for their air -fare, Passports and visa travel cards. Before you part with any cash you can check on

"The Russian Blacklist of Scammers"

You will see the identical professional looking pictures on that site.

Online Dating Safety!

Pay a Fee!….Is it safe?

True.com is the solo safest site! They do criminal background checks on all their members. It also checks if a person is married? If you state that you are single, when you are indeed married. True.com will take that person to court.

The free sites are enticing, how ever scam artists, felons and pure bad people cruise these sites without compassion to the person searching a partner.

Net addiction.

Instant messaging!

Avoid it. It is addictive.

Cyber crime!

The anonymity of the net has afforded "Con Artists" a new playground for scams. It allows people to be anyone they think you want them to be. The Internet dating scene is one of the easiest places for an individual to cheat on their spouse or partner and be promiscuous via a secret email address, create a persona and cheat from their chair!

Love Crosses the Pond.Com.

I dedicate this book to my friends around the globe of which there are many persuasions.

My D.C friends. Janice, Janet, Heather and Louis Who! have had me howling with laughter at their personal experiences at Internet Dating. A few experiences of mine were thrown in for good measure! The medicinal cocktails were flowing at Zorba's Bar in D.C. where we were swapping life experience stories at our personal expense from our faux paux's.

A few miles south to Florida and we have more friends that have experiences to yabba about and back to England where it appears I was a soothsayer to many Travelers that were transiting through the airports meeting up with hopeful sweethearts from around the globe! Whilst I was working at some of London's airports as a security agent!

Without the help of my many global friends I would not have so many life experience stories to tell on the experiences of Internet dating! It appears the world is infact a small place?

A Bitch is a bitch in any language and a Bastard speaks many languages?

For the nice people that do infect exist around the world.

"God Bless"

My introduction to "Internet Dating was from a co-worker.

We worked as mess manageresses at Prestigious Officers messes for the British Army! My friend Heidi was of German descent! Myself a typical English rose, We were different in nature, but nature is a wonderful teacher?

Several decades previously we would never have met?

Why?

War

Two world wars!

Which brought treachery and deceit, and not to like or trust our fellow men! How strange that a couple of decades later even though there are too many world wars to contemplate right now 2008! "People are engaging in world peace and love.

Trying to find love in any nationality"

It is happening! I saw this on many an occasion whilst I worked at the London Airports. Loves young dreams meeting for the first time at the meeting points!

Also!

Saying their farewells as they boarded their flights to different parts of the globe on their journeys back to their respective countries. There was always a tear!

Usually tears of happiness.

Power to the people who are brave enough to engage on their quest for love or friendship in any language.

CHAPTER ONE

The music is brash, yet subdued, a simple melody spun around an undulating bass line. Down tempo, jazz trip hop.

The Trio was unusual to a typical regimental style function. But this was a private function for my new commandant and I had to impress. My muse was constantly reminding me of my faux pas.

The Garrison was busy with a inter services boxing event All the messes were fully booked with functions and visiting dignitaries for the forthcoming boxing event.

" No room at the inn Ed…"

"My Officers Mess" with its newly commissioned Commandant was fully booked. The senior master at arms and guests were out to the "Boxing events".

The Royal Welsh Fusiliers who were guesting long term at my mess were out at the events and my muse was working overtime "you messed up big time….

"Watcha gonna do".

"Oh shut up, just shut up.

Can't shut up! I haven't got a mouth remember!

My universe collapsed around me the day I told the voice on the other side of the phone "so which part of no don't you understand".

My job, the responsibilities, The piametrical necessities, and with staff that would befit working in a nut house…..

Rosie the alcoholic bar maid come entertaining waitress with a hypochondriac illness "strapadicktome."

The officers usually had to give black coffee to Rosie at breakfast service whilst I cooked breakfast awaiting Stig of the dump the alcoholic chef to appear on duty.

I had to courier paperwork over to the Corps headquarters, on my way out of the officer's mess! Rosie called me, "Mam" that man is on the phone from Germany again. He wants a room in the mess tomorrow, "sorry I can't come to the phone". Tell him the officers mess is fully booked!"

On my return to the mess, "Mam that man is on the phone again from Germany he wants to speak to the mess manageress"

"Look Rosie just tell him we are full" I have to go back to the P.T. headquarters the PMC wants the accommodation plot file like yesterday.

"Mam he said his name is Ed".

"Tell him I said "What part of no does he not understand"

"Rosie make yourself useful tell him we are full"

On my return to the mess, Mam Ed is on the phone. He insists on talking to the mess manageress.

"Hello sir how may I help you"

"A room".

So sorry but the mess is full. "Sir"

"Yes sir we do have two rooms on the third floor".

One is for the senior master at arms, and the other room is for the Commandant of the Officers Mess P.T. Corps. !

This man is so insistent on a room I do not have.

"Would you like the room with the indoor pool sir"

Yes your outgoing Commandant has mentioned the room.

I kick back and absorb, But forget to engage my brain.

My oxymoron moment crept silently into my day.

My flight arrives from Germany at 0.900hrs tomorrow.

"Oh by the way your new commandant

Ruby

"Do you know his name"

.

"Yes sir it is Ed Mar……t…in…

Bollocks… Bollocks… Bollocks….

.

Prayer mat time!

My muse goes into overdrive. !

"You've done it this time" watcha gonna do?

"Shuddup.."

My life passes before me like an elevator falling down a lift shaft, "not doing so well are we muse mimics".

I know, I know!

I pontificate on my gaff.

"Sir of course your room is available for you, I will look forward to seeing you tomorrow"

"Bollocks"

The rile scope hit me hard. "What to do".

I phone my friend Gisela a mess manageress in an off garrison site.

Oh holy shit Gisela, my ass is grass tomorrow I told the new commandant he could not have a room in his own mess! Gisela in her German response… vwat? But zis, ju can no do Ruby

"I know this ".

You German Tart!

Of course the new commandant's room was already booked for tomorrow.

Gisela I was over at the P.T. headquarters with the P.M.C. doing the accommodation plot, this guy kept phoning and asking for a room," said his name was Ed" but not that he was the new Commandant.

anyway rambling Rosie was taking his phone calls, she was probably too pissed to engage her brain and ask what regiment he was in.

P.T. Corps may have given it away.

"I may be given away tomorrow Gisela".

I will be over straight away, I need to see your Q.M. "Really I said why do you need to see my Q.M. Gisela "?

Tell you when I see you.

Ciao.

"What Gisela"

Well last time I called in to see you, you had a closed door meeting with the army sports control board and the Q.M. was in the mess for his morning coffee…. So? Well we got chatting and he asked me out. "No! you German Jezebel.".

And did you go out?

"No"

Not yet!

But he phoned me at my mess and he said to come across here to your mess for a coffee, I was about to phone you anyway and tell you.

Don't worry about the Commandant he will be fine.

Anyway Ruby why don't you come over to my place tonight sounds like we both need a drink.

"So is there any man in your life yet Ruby"

Nah Gisela too busy and not that interested at the moment.

I have learnt what a remote control does now that I am single, You know there are more channels than just sport?

"Why don't you go on the Internet?

Try the online dating.

Gisela, that is so cheesy.

And full of "Fakes"

"Are you a fake Ruby"

"No"

I sign up and my life has never been the same since?

"Sniff Lauren"

I chose the strangest name on the chat room list.

He was single?

"An International banker"?

Gisela was on the cell to one of her many online Beaus'

She had gone international.

She was in giggle mode and whispering to me that this man she was chatting to wanted to take her to the opera in Vienna.

Lucky you say I.

Then another phone call this time from Amsterdam a customs officer Gisela had been chatting to earlier, Well maybe it is not so bad I thought.

Then Sniff Lauren asked for my telephone number, he wanted to hear my voice, click I removed him from my sight.

"You wuzz" Gisela said to me.

"Well" not so sure I wanted to speak to him.

"Come on Ruby we will go into the romance section Gisela said"

Gisela had several names she used on the chat room so she became.

"German Bombshell."

We hadn't been in the chat room too long before she got a visit or two.

"Want to see a pic".

Gisela was eager for the pics

She held a stifled giggle as the mega pixels were loading onto the screen.

She knew what to expect?

"I did not"

"I was in shock."

After the initial shock, I saw the funny side of the situ and Gisela and I ended up teasing the life out of the weirder on liners. I had guested on Gisela's computer so no harm done for me.

" I was unknown".

Gisela and I discussed how I would grovel to my new Commandant the following day. I drove home wondering if I should look at the situations vacant!

Like.

"Bat for him for ever says my inner voice"

I arrive at the mess extra early the following morning.

"Oh quelle surprise".

Rosie looking like Alice Cooper….

Hey Rosie that's clever how you get your mascara to run like that bit scary for breakfast though!

And the bed hair!

I slept in the staff room.

"Why Rosie"

"You know you are not allowed to do that"

The bar stayed open longer than usual Mam and I missed my bus!

"If Maria finds out you slept in the mess I will be on the carpet

"Rosie you are drunk"

Today of all days!

"Cheers".

"Well if you are offering I will have a brandy Mam.

"Cheers in the cheers thanks a lot sense Rosie and don't push your luck this is gross misconduct sort yourself out before breakfast service"

Where is "Stig of the dump"?

"Oh he is in the chefs office.

"Thank goodness"

A short lived "Thank goodness, Stig is nursing a mug of steaming coffee.

"Silly me"

Stig is nursing a mug of Brandy and staring into vacationland.

"Morning chef"

Everything under control then, "yes boss"

"Stig"

"Boss"

Fair exchange!

Today was not the day to "kick ass"

Help was required.

Maria my boss and site manager.

"Fucking Hell Ruby"

"I hope they do".

Seems that's where I will be going Maria.

"So what you are telling me is ".

Rosie is drunk ?……Yep.

Stig is drunk, Yep.

And you told the new commandant what part of no didn't he understand? and he could have the room with the indoor pool.

Errr , noooo, …. Err …Yes.

"Maria just letting you know my staff are inebriated," the Q.M. will be down for breakfast soon" I have to cook and set up the dining room too so I need you to come and hide Rosie and Stig until they sober up, before the Commandant arrives.

My boss Maria was not of a milquetoast nature.

I actually had an ace card, a secreted telephone number of the Garrison executive chef! He enjoyed a libation and was known to be unobtainable apart from his personal cell phone.

We had an occasion to have a much required drink after a severe bollocking from my P.M.C who had rubbished a luncheon.

"He had chosen the menu."!

We simply followed orders.

The luncheon was a disaster.

"Now there's a surprise"

The P.M.C was carpeted, so it simply followed suit that the executive chef and myself were jointly carpeted.

My reward for my silence on this matter was a secret phone number, of which I was

About to call in my favour.

Before I did this, Maria had to be put into the loop! Unfortunately keeping secrets was not her best feature. I would definitely be on the hit list for today.

The senior management were creatures of habit? Every morning they went to head office on the garrison, swapped their personal cars for company vehicles and chewed the fat with their bosses on any information to be shared. Then they collected company cell phones and swooped onto their respecting corps messes management.

I was obviously flavour of the day for Maria's venom.

"Sorry not today Maria".

Even my muse was telling me "Nice one Ruby"

I had already fixed the problem with regard to meals for the day after my phone call to schhh.

By the way Maria, you told me I had to have Rosie as my 2.I.C. the fact that you knew Rosie was an alcoholic was a bitter pill for me to swallow, after my hard work cleaning the Officers mess from lazy staff and gaining the officers respect.

"So Maria your shout"

Rosie is your problem.

She has run out of her nine lives with me, and committed professional misconduct on more than one occasion, however you choose to ignore that, I have guests to attend to so!

"Go Girl"

That was no muse saying that, I was like the proverbial "Cheshire Cat".

I punched the air in a victory "Up Yours!

"Maria you gotta see her," Blondie tune running through my head.

"Well maybe not"

Rosie was getting the roasting of her life, Maria was backpedaling for my benefit and hers too!

I asked Ruby to take you into her mess for me I felt sorry for you Rosie!

"This is a prestigious officers mess"and this is how you repay our kindness.

"Oh what's with the plural Maria I felt like saying.

I borrowed a waitress from Gisela's mess, her mess was for retired Generals so her waitresses were the best. " Old but the best"

On with the show!

Guests started to arrive, a lot of the guests were retired Army, some by choice others from long service.

Ed had three guests who were long retired from the army, They got the kiss ass treatment from me, and in return they gave me lots of information on "Ed"

My new commandant!

Ruby! Twenty five years ago Ed said to us!

"One Day I will be commandant of the P.T.Corps! in This Garrison".

The four of us served in Germany.

And here he is about to take over the mess.

"A word in your ear Ruby " he likes everything to be Rosie, and does not suffer fools gladly.

"Gulp"

Rosie? Could of chose a better word?

"How was I going to introduce Rosie".

This is Rosie my 2.IC sir, she looks after the dining room and bar in an extraordinary way! Likes to put a bit of a show on!

No

Sir" this is Rosie my 2.IC she has an illness, Strapadicktome, she tends to have a mattress on her back, but your officers have big smiles no!

"Stig Of the Dump".

"Sir"

"This is the officers mess head chef, he does not talk much... shell shock from the boar war. The boring war of me trying to keep him sober"

.

A warning from me to Stig? Breathe those alcoholic brandy fumes on the new Commandant and I will have a lucifer ready to set you alight caphiche!.

"Ed arrives" a phone call from the PM.C. "Ruby at the front door now! The Commandant has just left the school, he will be with you in five minutes."

I muster the staff, borrowed of course.

Stand alongside your mess Manageress Ruby at the front door Maria barks and no talking.

Any questions will be directed to your mess manageress Ruby! And answered by her is that understood…

Yes.

“Mam” Rosie is being sick in the gent’s toilet, "Maria I say you have to deal with it".

“Maria my muse mimics pay back time yeah.

Rosie may have permanent “Alice Cooper eyes”.

Not quite coming to America arrival, no rose petals, and certainly no personal bathing for Ed on the agenda. Unless Rosie gets loose? she is secured in my office no chance of that, sorry Ed.

Staff introductions are made to Ed, and staff are just as quickly shoed away to stand by.

Maria is on the Rosie and Stig de tox and I give Ed a tour of his mess, we will save the Regimental silver exhibit for another day Ruby Ed remarks, I have arranged a day and time with the Q.M.

Ed is shown his quarters and the friendly smile on the commandants face tells me all is not finished?I am the mouse and he is the cat.. Meow.

Luncheon served. Coffee served,speeches from Ed.

I held my breath I would like to thank the mess manageress for a splendid lunch. "Applause"gentlemen shall we retire to the bar? Phew

Safe in my office, Maria and I are now bravely laughing at the whole situation and Maria was going into over drive embellishing her thoughts on how the commandant would get me back”Really I said, and how are you going to get away with “Stig and Rosie”. who in their right minds would employ alkies?

“You are the mess manageress” deal with it!

Cocktail time.

Rosie scrubbed up well.

She had her moment of glory, it was her bar and dining room and some how she kept everything in order.

Stig had gone home, there were no Evening meals in the mess all were out to functions.

“Apart from Ed and his guests”.

Rosie could get where castor oil could not get! Ed was chatting to her, he was nobody’s fool and did not miss much.

Whilst they were chatting Ed’s three guests said so far we have had a lovely day thank you very much Ruby, We need to arrange something? We have these three jars filled with cockles, when we are at the bar later; empty the cockles into anything you wish and fill the jars with whiskey don’t even wash the jars, Then would you play?

"Whiskey In The Jar by Thin Lizzy"

"Ok".

As this was a private affair for the commandant and his guests, a very special occasion for the four of them to take a trip down memory lane from when they were sixteen-year-old recruits

I told the trio they could go home, the background music had created the desired ambience.

Rosie and I made the bar area available only to the Commandant and his guests.

Infact the Royal Welsh Fusiliers were told to stay away from the mess until the commandant gave permission for their return.

Chapter Two

Then Ed asked me to have a chat with him away from the ears of Rosie and his guests.

We sat in the ante room and the commandant said that he had been in a meeting at the school with the outgoing Commandant, the P.M.C. and the Q.M. before he came to the mess this morning. He had been briefed on the Mess and the staff, "that was a relief." Ed said the officers had a Pasha type of respect for me and the way I ran the mess! He was delighted I was his mess manageress, and he invited me to stay for his two year office with hi

I was very honored and said I would be delighted to stay at his mess. "So far so good". "No mention of my faux pas."

We returned to the bar, then the serious drinking began for the men.

Rosie and I were behind the bar listening to their stories, then we were invited to drink with them it was such a delight to hear the men reminisce.

Then Ed decided to tell his friends that they should not upset me, "why, s that Ed they chorused," well as you know this is now my mess and Ruby said I could not have a room. Nah she didn't.

"Did You"

"I was blushing "

It only took me twenty-five years to get the bloody thing and then she pissed on my parade and said "what part of no do you not understand,"

"Ed there is no room at the inn!"

"But " I could have the room with the indoor pool.

Runs a tight ship this lady does!

So I took a bow! The beginning of a very nice working relationship was cemented.

Then I produced the three jars of "Cockles" and Thin Lizzy was in the background as requested playing.

"Whiskey in the Jar".

"Ed actually looked astounded, Shocked? You could almost hear his memory button hit replay, twenty-five years of replay".

Then the four men were all talking in unison,

I had lit candles and had placed them on the bar and tables

Close your eyes make a wish! And blow out the candlelight, was very appropriate! At this precise moment, I did not want to make a sound, I was watching the men and they were quite emotional.

" For tonight is gonna be the night were gonna celebrate".

Boyz to Men As Thin Lizzy was playing they were for a few moments boy recruits again. Bless!

I sent Rosie home; no body was going to spoil the moment.

"They were gonna celebrate".

Then Ed took court, They were drinking fish flavored whiskey from the jars, the cockles were thrown aside? Ruby! Twenty five years ago we were serving in Germany, then they were all talking at once" No let me tell the story Ed said" Mutter, mutter, they all wanted to yak" So" We were in Hamburg and broke, yeah the guys chorused. "I had a date Ed said with a beautiful woman". Yeah the guys chorused! So! As we were broke and romance was the order of the evening, I had pulled first. A lot of laughter was now going on, and a few stories had slipped into the conversation about the knockbacks the other guys had got that evening twenty five years ago. So I escaped, quickly made a phone call to Gisela, I had promised to let her know how the evening was going?

Well very well actually Gisela, but I have had a drink! No problem Gisela said, don't worry! I will pick you up, you can stay at my place I have to be at my mess for six Am. so I will drop you at your mess first thing. Excellent give me an hour, I will phone the guard and tell them to let you on site.

I returned to the bar just in time to replenish the jars with whiskey, get yourself a drink mess manageress and come around to this side of the bar, that's an order.

"So Ed who it had been decided would narrate the memory lane story continued."

CHAPTER THREE

Yes Ruby we were broke and pooled our money! So I could take the lady to a Restaurant. I left these three to their own devices, I felt really good that I had enough money to impress and I was wearing this really cool long black leather coat, the waiter hung my coat up, stifled laughter is now going on with the other men and! they interrupted yeah was a nice coat!

Tee he

The meal was good and it was time to leave. Check please! "Excuse me I left

My wallet in my coat". My coat and wallet had gone? No way to impress my date

"And there was such a commotion, me being a British soldier pot less did not go down well with German Restaurant owner" My date left, I accused the waiter of taking my coat and wallet and I was thrown out of the restaurant".

Then these three show up and they are laughing so much?

"Why are you laughing", " you don't know what just happened to me"

Hey!

"Where did you find my coat"?

"Now it was the three guys that were holding court and telling me the story. "Well Ruby we were so mad at Ed, he took almost all of our cash and it was freezing.! We sat at a bar across from the restaurant and we had enough cash for a couple of beers. We watched him go into the restaurant and then when the waiter hung Ed's coat up! We ran across the road to the restaurant , we snook in and sped off with Ed's coat went back to the bar and sat and watched everything that happened in the restaurant.

When Ed came out of the restaurant we decided he had been punished enough for leaving us out in the cold, we were young and the plan was for us all to pull a girl so we then decided to go for a drink but everywhere was closed. Then we came across a bar that was just locking up and we pleaded and we were allowed to buy a bottle of whiskey at great expense may we add. “Any glasses mate” “No chance, “so then we came across a street vendor selling sea food so we bought three jars of cockles, because we only had enough cash for three jars of cockles.”

We emptied the cockles into a bin, then drank the whiskey from the jars. Ed got the bottle!

he has always been the lucky one?

That night we promised that if we were going out together we would all stay together and here we are all together again.

Now I understood why the commandant was so insistent on them being alone in his officers mess as the new commandant! for the evening without being disturbed.

How sweet!

The mess doorbell was ringing! so I went to the door. “It was the Welsh fusiliers” “permission to come into the mess please,”

They were hammered! The commandant appeared at the door, “Yes permission to enter my mess and gentlemen all of you to the bar no one is going to bed this evening”.

Oh Goodie

They would all fit in well with Rosie, at breakfast I did not have a worry.

I got a phone call from the security guards at the gate, Gisela had arrived, so I bagged a welsh fusilier and put him behind the bar. See you at breakfast I mouthed quietly, As I left I could hear the sounds of a Welsh choir. When I arrived at the mess at six a.m. I was greeted by the sounds of a Welsh choir.

The commandant would be away for two weeks so an early finish for me tonight!

Chapter Four

Gisela fancied a drink,” now there’s a surprise! That was definitely on my agenda. So over to Gisela’s place and we kick start the lappy.

“Gisela had been on line most of her evening, she was expecting a phone call from her “Vienna Man” as we had nick named him. He actually lived in Marseilles and was a music teacher," we went on line and as it was late there was not much happening on the U.K. romance. "so we went International. Ended up chatting to a faker in New Mexico," we could tell he was a young desperado and said we were going. He said he liked chatting to older women. Bet ya do we chorused to each other, so we had some fun with him, "so where is your wife" in the kitchen he replied so we asked if she knew he was in a chat room. "No he replied" so bet she is barefoot we said, he did not get that. So! we said, instead of chatting to us take your wife into the laundry room and sit her on the washing machine, put it on a fast spin cycle and have some fun." we clicked him into oblivion, see I said to Gisela told you the internet is full of fakes that was a young boy pretending to be a mature man"

We go back onto the U.K. .Fifty romance and "sniff Lauren is on" "you got company" so we decide to chat to him.

"Who am I chatting to", "Gisela or Ruby?" actually both of us and after a while I decided to go to bed, Gisela stayed on line a while longer and then her "Vienna man rang".

On the way to work the following morning, we both had a slight hammering going on in our heads so we pulled into the supermarket and got some Advil, give me my drugs now I pleaded to Gisela. Gotta have my drugs! The counter assistant gave us a strange look as we were fighting over the pack of pain relief capsules and giggling.

There were some complimentary AOL packs on the counter so we both took a couple and stashed them into our bags, when we finish work later Gisela said! We are going to your place and install the AOL on to your P.C. Ok! Nag, nag, nag, I said ok pushy.

"AOL up and running".

"See Gisela said cool aint it? Lets go onto fifty romance," she was away with the fairies. She was definitely having fun".

"Hey Gisela I said" "just a mo, " what ya up to you German tart" that is my name you are using. "Well right now you are chatting to "Mr69er"

"What I shrieked" Gisela was laughing so much, I had to see the funny side, well bump him off right now, I fed and watered us and then Gisela said.

"Oh by the way ".

"Whaat I said. "The look was enough from Gisela to say she had done something? I gave your email address to "Sniff Lauren" while you were just cooking dinner. When you went to bed last night he thought he was chatting to you, So he will definitely be getting in touch! He was gagging for it last night by the time I had finished. Wanted your phone number? "Don't worry, he does not have it" "gave him your address tho". "You may be having a visitor" " so will you from the grim reaper I replied".

Gisela knew better than to even think about doing such a dastardly deed, no man had crossed my threshold for a very long time! Apart from my Son, and Son In law. My friends were always winging for me but eventually gave up!

"Next time you use my p.c. you guest you German tart."

I was a complete novice at this ere im Stuff? And did not have a clue about 21st century dating protocol for upper middle class urban professionals, I was getting more dick head unprofessional, "You got company", want to chat! "Midnight mover asks" so I see you work for the Brit army? Me bored yep! And? ! So my inner muse voice was saying.

".What dress size am I, midnight mover asks? " I click him into cyber space.

"Told you! I said to Gisela, how is it possible to meet anyone genuine on line? could be talking to a woman pretending to be a man? "Did sniff Lauren get in touch Gisela asks".

" Yep he did, but I still do not know if he is single, married or what? I think he is a bit of a play away merchant with a wife stashed in the kitchen."

"Did he ask to take you out Ruby? "Don't be nosey" well did he Gisela asks again, "Well I suggested that you would be more of a willing dinner date so he will be getting in touch with you Tart".

"And sniff lauren did get in touch with Gisela, see told ya he was married I said, I had the last laugh Gisela said, he thinks he is taking us both out?

"That is what most of these people do in these ere chat circles, have fun at other peoples expense I said to Gisela, "Saves a fortune though, You don't have to go out to a bar and be insulted you can stay at home and get insulted for free, but at least some times it is entertaining. And so many ask the same questions."

"Like"

"Name three things you would take to a desert Island.".

"Not you three times is my usual response"

"Sir Prancelot," want to chat? I can't do this I say to my inner voice, "go on have some fun muse mimics, "take a walk on the wild side" "no you take a hike," I don't have legs or a mouth, I am just a disembodied voice that occasionally drives you nuts.".

"Occasionally"? Selling yourself a bit short now aren't we."?

"What dress size are you? Sir Prancelot asks."

"Heard you scream last night my neighbor states in the car park, nod, nod wink ,wink. Had company did ya."?

"No" have not quite got the hang of cyber sex yet I said!

Gisela had acquired a live in guest fresh off the internet! "Crazy lady I told her But good luck to you " Her new beau was indeed married and had escaped his wife of twenty years and peace reigned with Gisela and her man for quite some time.

Then, Gisela asked if she could use my p.c. sure you can, come on over, but behave

you tart I said. Gisela behave? not in this life time.

"How is your live in cyber lover I ask Gisela" Ruby he is so controlling and he has wiped out all my male friends from my p.c. "What a bastard I quip". And the nude photo's too I enquire? No that's "Esquire muse buts in. I just enjoy chatting on line but he won't let me.

Is "ta ta you control freak not in your vocabulary Gisela?.

"I ensure that Gisela is guesting on my p.c. and give her a bit of time to catch up with her cyber friends".

Then we have some catch up chat and drinks, after a few inquiring phone calls from control freak "Where are you." Think you had better go and save the peace Gisela. "I know but it's not fair I want to test all the waters! Gisela said." "You are such a tart I said to her " Gisela goes home to be controlled. Her guy wants Gisela to move to Sheffield Yorkshire several hundred miles away! This means she will be giving her job up and her home which is rented from a housing association and was not so easy to come by. Gisela wanted to be happy! So we weighed up the pro's and cons and as much as the guy was controlling he had made Gisela a very happy woman, wined and dined her. Took her on romantic holidays and introduced her to his friends in Sheffield.

Gisela decided to make a go of it and decided to move! So the following day she was going to give her notice to leave her officers mess! Things were changing, I also had made a life changing decision concerning my officers mess? Much to my commandants disbelief at the fact I would be leaving him!.

There was too much going on at the officers mess? I had been too good at making a clean sweep as mess manageress for a couple of years. I had uncovered a couple of scams that my managers were trying to cover up?. They were in serious trouble with the army and my P.C who backed me up a thousand percent was ready to call in Whitehall? The accounts were being messed with! Due to the accountants!? Which the management were trying to cover up! I had uncovered this and clearly had to go to save the management's sorry asses!

I was made an offer I could not refuse by a kangaroo court made up of the offending management As long as I remained silent on their scams? I could not inform my commandant! Or, any army personnel?

I was returning to work at the airports, and looking forward to it.

I am a great believer in. "What goes around comes around.."

I noticed that Gisela had left my p.c. running, It had been returned to my user name? Hello who is this? A bio page mm he sounds nice.

"Gentleman Jack" and how interesting what a pleasant change! "Go on muse says he sounds nice. "For Once I Agree"

" I had just recently returned from Florida visiting friends that had lived as my neighbors in Vero Beach! This ere "Gentleman Jack was across the pond". Nah he is probably, probably what muse asks? Go on!, I decide to be brave and write a short message.

A couple of days later, a reply, a pleasant reply! " Oh my gosh".

"Gisela"! Gentleman jack wrote back!

So write back to him! I had just about given up being able to write to anyone nice, I am still a novice at this! Just answer his mail.

How do I respond? And hopefully solicit a response? This is worse than a blind date! I am getting butterflies in my tum and I am in the comfort of my own home!

A response.! Gentleman Jack likes my profile, This puts a click in my heel! I dance, and sing and do silly things. Pics have been swapped! We like what we see?

Gentleman Jack is a musician! This gets better by the minute? I had been married to a musician and we had been in the entertainment Industry, we had something in common to converse about!..

Chapter five

He said he was off to Philly on a gig with his band and said he would be in touch on his return after the Weekend.! I detected from his manner that he was an Intellectual person?. Gentleman jack kept his word! He wrote to me and we did the bio stuff? He appeared to be quite interested in the fact I worked at the airport for the major American Airlines and I was a Profiler! I worked for a Security company that had contracts from the American Government securing safety for American airline carriers through an FBI program whereby I had to pass several exams, which then placed me onto the FBI system, meaning I was on the FBI hit list!. We started to instant message! He was so obviously into cyber chat, " Me "I was such a novice! On one occasion he asked me how my pooter was? I assumed he meant my P.C so I said it was a computer that I had shipped back from the States when I lived there? If I knew then what I now know I would have died of embarrassment.? I guess he liked the fact I was rather naïve? . Who Knows? Lets hope so!. I started work at five am at Gatwick airport! I had to be up at three am, so with the time difference of five hours in the U.S! This meant we talked before I left for work. Then we would chat when I returned from work. I assumed because he was a Musician he had a lot of free time in between gigs?

NEVER ASSUME!

We exchanged lots of information on instant messaging! It was addictive, I would chat about the airport and use flight lingo! I had been years earlier a flight Attendant, the airline industry is something that always stays with you! He understood the flight lingo but stayed covert? He was concerned that the current state of affairs, bombing's at airports etc me dealing with the type of security I was handling? Constantly taking exams on higher security and being in the program I was in? I should have picked up from his conversation that he was not just a musician? I had to take another American security exam that required a couple of weeks of serious revision!, so I mentioned that I would be keeping a low profile and may not be on line for a couple of weeks. Gentleman Jack said he had some business to attend to and that he would also not be around for a while. On his profile, one of JD's hobbies was "Ghost Hunting". I lived in a haunted building. Really, It was a converted pub so we had a lot in common on that topic. I passed my exams and was eager to let JD know, but he was not around? He was so covert. I thought I had maybe been rude when i said that i needed time for my exams?. In retrospect may be I had been selfish?. A few minutes to say hi would not have taken up too much time would it. There was a tight bond of friendship through the instant messaging! Some where in my distant foggy memory I recalled that JD had said that "All would be revealed" he had already touched my heart strings by telling me why he was single.? not married? Never mentioned if he did, or did not have a Partner? Lady friends of course were in the equation.

Instant messaging had taken a hold on me and it was like a drug!

Or was it the man?

One minute we were chatting almost every day! Then a whole month went by and no signs of JD. " Maybe JD was off on a "ghost hunting expedition"?

I decided that "Sniff Lauren may be deserved a date? He had been emailing me and I had been ignoring him! Yes because of JD but JD was so exciting.

He was charming, witty, a sense of humor to have you splitting your sides laughing. He was very caring and had a private side to him that I had been invited into by way of some help that he had offered to me when I was in so much despair with the haunted building I was living in! That I cherish with so much fondness that I was allowed into his other world of Tsalagi and I knew the other Tsalagi people he had asked to help me were very Honored people.. It was such an honor even for him! And for me one I will always cherish. I was a babbling Brit wreck in a haunted pub, no Tsalagi blood in me but his people came to my rescue for which I am eternally grateful, and for the non-believers…Don't even go there!

If you ever get a Boo in the night! Start believing?

"I AM GRATEFULL!

Cyber Date.

Sniff Lauren International Banker?

So! Can I have your phone number? I caved in. We had been emailing for about three months!. I gave him my cell number and he rang me quite a lot! Cheeky chap asked if we met up would I wear certain apparel?

Stockings!

I chilled away from him and basically said I was looking for a relationship, not a night of fantasy with a married man!

I had now been single for a couple of years, Stupid me thought that if the guy said he was single. He was single?

Oh how they lie!

So! Onwards and forward….Next?

"Sir Prancelot?" Where do they get these names.?. Fantasy land me thainks!

It is possibly a give away that they are married men playing away games, or we can believe them when they say they are single. It s a game of chance. Even if you met a guy in a bar it would be the same. A Chance! We chat and exchange phone numbers! Because of the nature of my work and the early hours I need to be up. My social life is a bit of a roller coaster ride!

When Sir Prancelot realizes I work at gatwick airport, he mentions that I must pass his gaff every day on my journey to and from the airport. We must arrange a date? He is very attentive with his phone calls, I arrange to meet him on my journey home from work. It is hardly out of my way!

A quick detour off the M25 and an arranged meeting point. It is early afternoon and a hot summer's day!

I had changed out of my uniform, thank goodness?

His car pulled up alongside mine at the lay by we had arranged to meet at! He wound his car window down gave me a wolf whistle and a wink!

Follow me, and his car sped off.

What is it with female? We are our own worst enemies! Because he said follow me! A male directive, He was off in a cloud of dust I followed.

As I followed I noticed that the number plates on his car were "Personal" His name was Lance which explained the sudonem! We arrived at his pad! A rented apartment?

A quick tour of his place and a pointed double viewing of his boudoir! Along with a Cheshire cat grin!

* * *

It was so hot!

Would you like a drink? Lancelot asks! Yes I reply! A stiff drink my inner voice quips!

Would you like a wine?

Wine?" He Wants Me To Wine? This is freaky. Oh a glass of wine, ok sure. I am like a cat on a hot tin roof. Very uncomfortable!

We will have to go to the shop to get some wine! It is just across the road. Lance has an extremely broad Yorkshire accent? Just for conversation I mentioned that I had a friend that had re-located to Sheffield, t hat was his hometown! What a co-incidence. Lance had me in a bear hug as we crossed the road to the shop, my feet hardly touched the ground as we crossed the road! Once inside the shop the bear hug was slightly released to a round the neck hold. I think he liked me!

The cold chiller cabinets in the shop were not working? Over worked from the extra hot weather we had been having Lance explained! He plucked a bottle of the cheapest tackiest white wine from a shelf as if it was a bottle of expensive champagne? This do lass? In his broadest Yorkshire accent. And a yo ho me hearty grin!. I attempted a Spanish shrug?

Back at chez Lancelot's pad in the kitchen! A couple of slim Jim glasses were produced, hmm, wine ……wine glasses usually!

Take that silver spoon out of your mouth my inner voice reminds me!

The slim Jim glasses remain and a large measure of slightly hot wine is handed to me! I just know I am about ready to "Toss my cookies" if I even attempted to drink this hot libation!

I politely ask if I could have some ice?

Put thice in wine lass? Lance has broken into even broader Yorkshire dialect, thice in wine yer canna put thice in wine Lass?

"Accents". Are they important?

Would I rather be in the arms of a beautiful man whispering amatevi bella Madonna into my neck as he was seducing me with a chilled glass of bubbles ?

Then the answer is YES.

I have decided that Lance is not only lacking in "Social graces" he is infect a "Pikie" decked out in the uniform, lots of heavy "Bling" Fairground style jewelry.

I am then subjected to a photo album session of Lance in his early years!

He was a long distance lorry driver, he employed a couple of drivers now etc yadda, yadda, me, me, me.

" I suppose I had better feed ya lass"? It was still early, around six p.m. The curry house will be open now Lance quipped! I will just go over and get a take away. Take us away my inner voice pleaded

Lance returned with the curry and placed the packages on the coffee table! He returned with some cutlery…My face must have been a picture when Lance realized as he had company maybe eating from the cartons was not on my agenda!

Oh Posh cow, suppose I had better get some plates?

I had been planning my escape? Lance had returned from the take away in break neck speed!

The plates were produced! and just as the cartons were opened some of the curry escaped from the box. Lance decided to lick the escaping sauce from the carton, and then he spooned the contents between our plates. I had lost my appetite and made polite noises about maybe! I would eat the curry later? Minus **The Saliva,** conversation was slightly still! me, me, me from lance. His wife had rang him about some business that needed discussing, thank you God! My escape. " So you are still married lance I asked"?

Well! yes but I live here on my own! My wife has the house, and she does my business accounts and banking. She likes to keep the accounts. "Oh really! don,t mess woman then!" I am not very good at doing the accounts. Never heard of an accountant I want to ask?

Well I must leave lance! I have to be up at three am. Don't you have your uniform with you lance asked? No I Lied! That's a shame you are halfway to the airport from here! you could have stayed! Maybe next time lance said.

Not in your fucking dreams mate. I was halfway to the door! When Lance asked if I would see him at the weekend. Muse was saying faster, faster before he puts the lips on you gal. I was taking the steps two at a time and lance was hot on my tail

Bang! The front door closed behind us!. He was locked out and he threw a Tantrum!

I jumped into my car and did not wind the window down? No chance of him putting his head through the window for a farewell kiss! The mood I was in it would have been an Israeli kiss?

Then I made a hasty retreat from Chez Prance'alot's.

I was lost and almost out of gas! Out in the sticks driving through forestry. I came across a traffic roundabout and saw a car coming from my left. I blocked the car and asked for directions to the motorway? Lucky for me it was a young man and he told me to follow him, he was heading that way.

I arrived home and deleted "Sir Prancelot " from my Email.

Another married man masquerading as a singleton!

Once again I realized just how dangerous this inter-net dating was? I was too trusting a person and needed to wake up!. Hey but I was being honest in my approach!. Single lady!, giving a full bio page and what I was looking for?

Not Mr. Wonderful! Just an honest nice guy looking forwards to some happening! Nice times lets face it some of us are! speaking for myself! Fifty plus, and if we like it or not as much as we have looked after ourselves and do not actually look our ages and could pass for a handsome looking forty year old, we are what we are!

"BEAUTIFUL PEOPLE."

With a history? Probably been married? Maybe not! Maybe children, maybe not! Does it matter?

History should be Just that! And if we are big enough and strong enough to look forwards to meeting new Beau's why should history be so important? Baggage? Yep got loads of it at my age? What you gonna do?

"Read and weep"

Or get a brand new life and move on?

Da, da, da da, da da!

We are in at our age group in our!

"Own Personal Summers"

Why? Do guys reach an age group of lets say "When they Pass Eighteen"

Do men ever pass eighteen?

Men are always in "short trousers"

But hey! Women obviously adore short trousers!

Men at any age want.

"Arm Candy"

They get married, Then divorced, reach the tender age of fifty, Fifty plus. Go on the "Internet dating"

Men!

So! What type of woman are you looking for?

S.B.G.LS.OH. 35...45, F.E.N.G.B.J.sw….doesnot….s.pit?

Get a life guys, you probably just left the best woman you ever had in your life. The romance died a little, who's fault was that?

Ok. Maybe you have a story to tell? Pray tell we love a good story?

At our age why can't we just let it "Be"

The make up Bio pages, Lie and you will stay single?

man 51, average build! Would like to meet a woman 30/35.

Wake Up!

When you were actually thirty to thirty five years old you could not get a date with a thirty to thirty five year old woman?

So now you are fifty years old! At the Prayer Mat looking for the woman of your dreams? But she has to be between the ages of thirty, to thirty five?

For the beautiful women in their own personal summers of Fifty plus.

We have our own stories to tell of course?

So we get brave and put out our bio pages on the dating agencies.

Only to find that the men in our supposed age groups think we are past our sell by date!

How rude these men are!

Because! We are, what we are? Can't change it Fifty plus!

We are looking for some Prince Charming.

Some one to spend some quality time with and have some good honest fun! It appears that the men in our supposed age group are living in fantasy land, away with the fairies want a Barbie doll to play with?

Oh dear guys! You Do So Obviously Not Know What You are Missing!

Most women at the age of fifty, that have looked after their appearance and could easily pass for a late thirties early forty! Well silly you! guys. These women are probably just what you are looking for? Thing is we have stated quite honestly that we are in the age category that we are!.

It appears that we are categorized from men as a no go! But possibly as we are so old.

Ok for a guaranteed shag for one night!

Why?

Because! Silly! Because!, we are so grateful?

Oh? And why is that? We are hopefully chatting to men of a similar age group are we not?

Apparently not so! La la land is where these men are living!

They obviously have not met me!

I would love a Salsa, but me being me do not come so cheaply! I am unique! I have not had a Salsa for a while, too many years, schhh. They broke the mold when they made me? I truly believe I am named the original virgin mary.

I would love to live in La la land and create a perfect man.

For me?

Someone! that would not be a control freak, possibly worked in an industry that involved being apart for a while. After the control freak I had escaped in my traumatic marriage!

Gentleman jack appears on my computer screen! Whoosh, Just like that! Hmmm know there's a thought!

Hi Honey I'm home! xxxxxxxxx. Mwaahh

Bless the bastard! is what I feel like saying! But politeness, experience and just glad to see him around experience taught me to be totally honest?

I was so happy to see him albeit on a P.C screen.

Covert! I had now re-named JD. Sure JD would always be remembered as JD. Just like the drink? Strong! And powerful? Depended how much you embibed?, Could be Heaven or could be hell? Depended how much you cared to partake!

This man flew by the seat of his pants?, literally!.....oh swing my pants!

Covert had been involved in a chopper crash and had been hospitalized, hence no contact!.

Covert had decided to update his bio page with me? Helicopter? Are you with the military I asked? Covert already knew my son Jake was an ex chopper pilot. Plus he knew any info was safe with me! all my details were on some database in Virginia USA.

When I realized what Covert did actually do for Uncle Sam I decided the glass of water I was drinking would be better poured over my head!

Covert named his partner in crime pilot Crazy Diamond.

Covert had mentioned CD on lots of occasions? So it now made more sense to me. They were both crazy?

Thank Goodness!

Thought It was just me?

I had nicknamed JD Mr. Cosmopolitan! on lots of occasions when he had been on the Missing List? Along with CD! his partner in crime?

The usual response was .Yep been travelling! Usually Iraq!

Covert and I had upgraded to telephone conversation, which was really exciting! I thought I already knew Covert? How wrong I was! Now I knew Covert was with the military! The other woman in his life!

I assumed that the other woman in his life was music? Ok so he had two women in his life?

And of course his partner in crime pilot Crazy Diamond

Covert was relating a story about CD's latest low altitude flying some where in Iraq! it went something like? .Stop it just stop singing shine on you crazy diamond to which CD sang an elongated version of shiiiine on you crazy dimon hoo boy yehhh.

Covert had his head in his hands pleading no more pink Floyd perleaaaase! Then he heard a delicate sound of thunder. Well it sounded like thunder? Heck no it was cd flying under a bridge instead of over it! Whoooop, whoop, covert screamed at cd so!. I train you aviation personnel on the meteorological impacts on aviation and ground equipment per se! for operation in total threat environment?. cd answered with another elongated version of shiiiine on.

cd was having an away day! Much to the total surprise of covert, "cd said I am so bored of browning techniques,whiting in this hell hole is not possible! So I thought I would try blueing, water would be so refreshing right now".

Over and out!

As we were chatting I had remembered that I had been explaining airline lingo to Covert on quite a few occasions! When we had been instant messaging.

I wished for a hole so I could jump into it, but Covert being the jokey Hawkeye character of Mash movie fame that he was! Decided to leave it on a funny!

Covert aka hawkeye was convalescing and would be home for a while!.

Until his next jolly!, with cd.

Ye Gads!

He was going to New Orleans to a music festival with his band! Sugarland Run!

A Militry Band!.coooooool

The venue never took place?

The big easy fell to a devastating disaster!

Covert and cd spent their next few months in the big easy controlling the disaster!

We chatted every day they were in New Orleans until they both safely returned home for some r& r JD to his usual? Cd to his lovely wife and children! then back to the sunshine state of Iraq!

.

God bless the mad pair! And they're respective partners!

Chapter Six

Next!

Ok, Ok, personal info here!" Sniff Lauren convinced me he was going through a divorce? He was sorry he had asked me to wear stockings on a date with him! He was just a cheeky chap! What do you think?

We arranged to meet at a local pub close to where I lived. It was a lovely Summer's evening, I sat outside the pub in the beer garden. Cell phones at the ready, the man walking towards me chatting on his phone appears to be the man I was waiting for?

Hello was not in my conversation, I looked at "Sniff Lauren"

So? "How old was that photograph you sent to me I asked him". Even I had to tell myself off for being so rude, but he had been deceitful

He gave a cheeky laugh. A few years old, actually four years old!. It was taken in New York when I left International Banking.

Ah? So! you are not an International banker then. No not any longer I teach football now! International Banking sounds better on the old chat lines.

Were you ever an International banker? I asked! Oh yes! And with that opener I listened to Sniff Lauren's stories of when he lived in New York, the places he missed over there in the "Big Apple "we swapped stories on New York? It had been my second home when I was a Flight Attendant. Toronto and Montreal too. How different living standards were in the uk. We agreed that England is a very expensive country to live in! Swapped places of interest we had visited in N.Y.! Montreal and Toronto and had a chat about that!

It was getting dark in the beer garden! We went inside to the restaurant but Sniff Lauren decided that he was not hungry. It appeared that I was "Dinner.

How rude!

I had decided he was not on my personal menu! If he had of been I would have been a "Willing Desert" Such a tart? But hey I am past my sell by date, and as much romance is supposed to be in the air! As much as my mother taught me to cross my legs! On a first date. My first date was thirty plus years ago. Did it still count now?

YES!

I am in a dilemma! "Sniff Lauren realizes I am not such easy meat and orders some appetisers!

I excuse myself and go to "Powder my Derriere!"

My salvation lies in a neighbor that is partaking of a libation at the bar, and as I pass by him and pass "a pleasant good evening to him" go to powder my nose return to pass the bar, and my neighbor is just departing! Night Ruby Goodnight Laurie! Hey?, I had a thought? Would you mind giving me a lift home? We lived in the same apartment block, the converted pub. Yep no problem, No probs Ruby, it's not a good idea for you to walk along the Basingstoke canal at this time of night!. You ready to go now? yeh!

I being me was worried about being polite! Actually why was I being so nice? "Sniff Lauren" thought I was his "Dinner"How rude.

Chatting to him for a few months gave him the god dam right to think.

A night away from his Wifey, plus the fact I had been single for a few years and had not dated he could "Rock my boat".

Ta, Ta, to Sniff Lauren!

Once safe indoors i got the teat on the bottle of wine and played some tunes!.

Gabrielle…All By myself.

Not for long my neighbor Maggie came to the rescue! The tunes changed to Chaka Khan I'm every Woman! Ending on a rendition of It's raining men?

Not quite sure where,? But the music was lifting the moment.

We had both decided to rent out our apartments, the constant interest rate increases to our mortgage rates, thanks to the bank of England which is so apparently running this country! Not our government as the rest of the world appears to think. So we made plans for that to occur sooner rather than later. The following day we both had people viewing our places. Maggie had her ex husband as a lodger? Turned out he decided to tell Maggie after two children and twenty years of marriage that he was gay! Honesty can be cruel and painful some times.

They divorced and remained friends, hence her ex hubby lodging with Maggie and her second husband! Her ex hubby Ralph had found an apartment and was moving out, Maggie's absent husband was in Guyana? She was thinking of divorcing him too! That is another story!

Ralph moved out the following day, and Maggie and i got our Tenants for our apartments. They were not my first choice of Tenants. They were Zimbabweans and did not have any references apart from family?

There was a lot of Zimbabwean people in the area! Working mostly in the care industry.

Ralph called around to see me before he moved out of Maggie's completely.

Could he possibly use my P.C? his was over at his new place and not connected!

Dajavus!

Hey i am not complaining.. I had found Covert from some one using my P.C. and Covert and I had developed a really nice friendship.

Do you have a mike and a headset Ruby? Yeees? I got the gadgets for Ralph and he asked if he could go onto Yahoo chat? So i then got into chatting to Ralph about yahoo. We got the chat up, it was all new to me! There were lots of headset icons, and mike icons. Ralph was trying to remember how to get onto the chat and put the headset on my head so I could hear people chatting. He pressed a key? I was talking to Ralph but unbeknown to me I was also chatting to a group of people. I realized this when a guy said hey who's that with the plummy accent? I said my name and I pulled the headset off quickly and gave it to Ralph. He then started to chat but to the same group of people. The same guy said hey! Ruby's voice has changed? Ralph was howling with laughter, he put the headset back on my head and i chatted to the same guy who was also seeing the funny side of things when I explained. I was not into chat rooms, basically because it was for seasoned chatters? And I was still not into instant messaging jargon? ..brb? Covert and I were! on one occasion chatting, he messaged brb and disappeared for a couple of minutes! It took me one of those minutes to realize what brb meant…….Blonde or what!

There's more?

I also thought that when I was online and I got the!

Youv'e got company, Covert would appear on my Buddy list!

I thought I had to contact him? He had appeared on my Buddy list to personally chat to me!

Whoops! he was very polite about it.

I decided to give the internet dating malarky a wide berth for a while!

My friends and family obviously had other plans for me. I had been on my own too long they had decided?

I was now living with my Daughter Laura and Son-In law Dennis and their Daughter

Ok Mother! where is your purse? I need your credit card?

Laura had decided to put me onto GMTV dating. They knew I would not attempt to try any more dating. And so it happened that they got to choose men for me, they got hooked on the whole dating scene! it was hilarious they would choose some one and show me. The bio stuff ! err ,no! Thank you but no thanks!

I never actually tuned into it. I did not get a chance? The PC was in my bedroom and either Laura or Dennis would be checking to see who was interested in me? Then my Daughter Christine would check and my son Jake visited on one occasion and where did we find him? In my bedroom checking out the men that had written to me. They were all hooked on it!

Borislav! from Moscow, Russia. I have one daughter and I would like to marry you. I do not drink alcohol Well I do so Borislav off!

The kids were having fun with my possible Beau's.

It all came to an abrupt halt. Via a virus that decided to eat my file! ,plus my ex husbands files on his PC.. Jake had sent his father an e-mail from my computer! He was in the music industry and had some valuable content stored. Had being the operative word!

That stopped the online poker games too, my ex was well into Poker games and so were Laura and Dennis. Think of the money you are saving I said?

I did feel bad about the virus! But it had stopped the winging that they had been attempting at with me and a Beau!

Did It?

What about the Pilot's at the airport where you work?

Will you lot give it up!

What about the pilots? Yep there's lots of them at the airport.

My friends and family were only trying to help!

It was me? .

I was not ready to trust a man again especially after my attempts at Sniff Lauren and Sir Prancelot.

They were after all married!

If the weather was too bad to drive to gatwick, i would get the fast train to the airport from a local train station that was walking distance from my home.

Well running distance?

After all I was leaving home in the dark early hours, This particular morning an urban fox decided to cross my path, I gave a loud piercing scream and cursed the management company that we paid an extortionate amount of money to for the upkeep of the building, including exterior lights that did not work?

Well one light at the side of the building came on for three seconds?

A whole three seconds!.

Maggie and I had timed it. If we went out for a drink in the evenings on returning!

When the outside light on the building used to stay on for a whole sixty seconds! We would do spotlight singing and dancing?

The game plan was you had to sing as many words to a song before the light went out. And dance like the Pink Panther.

I guess the neighbor who controlled the lights timer decided enough was enough?

After the piercing scream! And no Sir galahad, Maybe the neighbors thought I had finally mastered the art of Cyber sex it was after all three thirty am. I run to the train station, catch the train and arrive at the airport. Go to the ops room and see which American airline I am designated to today?

Muse is giving me a hard time?

They're gonna give ya Delta, ah shaddup

North terminal! a dead give away.

Delta.

There is absolutely nothing wrong with the airline!

It was the two destinations.

Atlanta, and Cincinnati?

Returning American citizens to these destinations appeared to be?

Bible Bashers

I would go over to the north terminal set up the departure snake with my colleagues and we would have a bet who got the first.

Praise the Lord.

Large groups of choirs and church groups appeared to return to these two destinations of

Cincinnati and Atlanta.

We would enter the snake and ask as profilers! The mandatory questions set down by the American homeland security. These questions were lengthy, had to be verbatim and there were also other security procedures we had to follow.

One particular English lady was quite reluctant to answer the questions? when she was informed she would not be allowed to board the flight if she did not answer the mandatory questions? She decided to tell me that she was travelling to Atlanta to meet a man she had met on the Internet, and she was slightly embarrassed? I was not allowed to enter into a Private Conversation with airline travelers, unless I got a search on her?

I did this, which allowed me time to basically set her at ease, and check out her story to satisfy security.

I got the chance to ask more in depth questions which was the norm if you pulled a pax out of the snake.

We managed to swop email addresses.

She promised to e-mail me to let me know she had arrived safely and that everything was ok with her and her new beau?.

I finished my shift and waited for my train home. The platform was busy and being in uniform it was clear I worked at the airport!

A man was trying to give me eye contact.

He was quite good looking and very tanned? Not unusual at the airport!

The train arrived and I boarded, the man followed me and asked if he could sit next to me?

He chatted about his work and the fact he lived in Spain, was in England to see his parents and they lived in Farnborough.

Just before we got to our destination he asked?

Could he take me out?

I agreed and allowed him to collect me from the car park of the building I lived at! .

Trusting.

I am far too trusting.

Silly Gal?

My date waited on the car park!, rang my phone to say he was outside? Which he was, I went outside to meet him, then he asked if he could use my bathroom?

What could I say?

No! would have been the correct answer?

Inside my place off he goes for his jimmy riddle.

Then I answer my phone so whilst I do this cheeky chappy sits down and starts to look at my music collection! Then after I finish my phone call he asks if I have anything to drink?

I thought we were going out?

You have some excellent music! Do you mind if I listen to The Darkness.? I think Justin Hawkes is cool.

Justin Hawkes is cool….Ok. I am not so sure about you! I decided as I was in my own home I was not going to be bullied.

Muse agreed. .Go girl, tell him!

I did offer the guy a drink he seemed to be half apologetic,.Can't blame a man for trying etc. He was married.

Did not want to be seen around town with a new woman!

Boo hoo…I give up!

Well I did not Give it up. I said he had to leave.

What a shame! he was a Rod Stewart look alike.

Back at Gatwick the following morning!

The ops room had a notice for personal who would be willing to transfer to Heathrow for the Summer?

There's a thought?

If they say Delta I will consider that option.

I could not take another day of "Praise The Lord"

Or? The Delta Dawn rendition?

Continental.gate fifteen.

South terminal!

I had worked that gate a few times for Continental and it was one of my favourites because of the routes.

New York myself and other personel met the flights on arrival and once the passengers had disembarked, the ground crew boarded and the departing flight crew and Air Marshal would have a chat. The Air Marshal had to wait for the Police to secure their guns and usually there was coffee and whatever food was left would be distributed around the ground crew!

Strangely enough Covert did some work for Conti, I did not ask what?

I would imagine air marshalling tho!

So here we were both working for the same airline.?

Betweent the pond?

Well on an odd occasion?

Small world!

...

Talking off which.......

Covert had been involved in another accident?......He obviously adored

Hospital Food?

The next contact I had with Covert was during the Hurricane Season that the States have more than their fair share of!

Covert and cd were off to the Big Easy.

New Orleans had fallen and there was a lot of help required from people of all persuasions!.

Covert and cd were kept busy there and after New Orleans we lost touch for a while?......

Covert had gone Covert? Covert and cd were probably in Iraq

I sort of knew the signs now!

I had not got over The Tsunami tragedy! I arrived at Gatwick airport on the 27th December.

To get to the ops room, you passed the airport chapel which was usually empty!

It was full of Heart broken People. So many different clergy?

In the ops room I was told that gates fifteen to seventeen that I usually worked for Conti were tightly secured and the blinds drawn. For respect of the dead!

I went to the pier and searched out where the Continental Newark flight was being sent to?.

It was so sad to see the passengers returning from the ordeal of the Tsunami!.

The amount of differing clergy was amazing to see down at the gates waiting for the mercy flights to arrive!

They needed extra security on the Tarmac so a lot of us had to go out there?

Extra aircraft were landing with the mercy flights coming in with the Tsunami victims. At this point I did not realize that a personal friend of my Daughter and Son-In Law, and therefore someone I knew was a victim!

Sort of gives you a wake up call?

Big Time!

I had decided to move to Heathrow airport much to the dismay of my co-workers who were attempting to dissuade me from moving to Heathrow.

You will not like it there?

We worked there last summer and it is not run so smooth as here at Gatwick?

Really!

I found that hard to believe?

At Gatwick, we were named as Gatwick airport workers.

Carrot Crunchers!

Gatwick was quite close to the country and coast, hence the nick name!.

I listened to some of the bad stories from my co-workers about working at Heathrow but my mind was made up!

I would be transferred to Heathrow in the next couple of weeks!

* * * * * * * * * * * * * * * * *

Chapter Seven

The aroma of curry was strong, The music was Hindu, cell phones had popular Bollywood ringtones.

The chat was in lots of different Indian dialects and loud.

I was the only flaxen haired rosie cheeked person in the room.

I attempted speak to the man in charge?

. . . .

It was the ops room at Heathrow. I had reported for duty!

This was different?

I was assigned to a team.

United Airlines…Pick up a Barringer machine and take it to gate twelve? For the Washington D.C. flight.

A barringer machine? What pray tell is a barringer machine.

The United crew were inside the gate.! The doors were securely closed and passengers queuing outside. The usual safety checks had been done and the gate and aircraft had been sanitized.

I was assigned to open the doors and stand at a podium to check passports.

The gate opened and all hell let loose, It was like being in a street market in downtown Deli. The agents were shouting across to each other in their varying dialects, I was in shock? The supervisor was just as bad, shouting back at the agents in Urdu. Some of them were chatting on their cell phones?

I was still the only flaxen haired rosie cheeked agent at the gate! I gave a Spanish shrug to the United captain and flight crew who had noticed my astonished look at the scene going on.

Once the flight had departed the plan was to go to another gate for the next Washington flight. I was the new girl so a lot of questions were fired at me from the co-workers.

What is it like at Gatwick airport they wanted to know?

Protocol!.i decided had to remain. Gatwick airport was much tighter run, our company ATCS had strict rules that we had to adhere to no cell phones at the airport gates all. Conversation was to be spoken in the international flight, airport code of English. I knew that I was dealing with a different type of personnel here?

Hierarchy called!

I was requested to assist with a security? A false passport was about to be used on the next D.C flight?.

I was sent to land side to assist with a security procedure dealing with the false passport?.

It was hectic at the check in!

Myself and one other United agent at either side of the check in snake! Walkie-talkie's at the ready. It was the New Year rush home to the states for most of the visiting U.S citizens and a few extra business people etc and other pax.

We as two sole agents had the conversation. It's just the two of us.

There's a song somewhere?

We prayed to the Almighty.

Please do not allow any Oddballs, Suspicious passengers, asylum seekers, to jeopardize the search for this one passenger we were trying to apprehend.

We had the nationality of the offender, just please no other offenders, we needed to catch the man?.

I spotted the couple first?

My muse was in hysteric mode? Whoo hoo you got first prize.

I was asking the almighty to make them go away.. Go away! come back another day.

Off you go and don't come back.

08.00 hours,! Woman in full length fur coat! Blinged up with all the trimmings!.

Her partner dressed like "Bob The Builder", muddy boots to impress! Looked as if he had stepped of a building site.

The female pax was giving all the signs of a suspicious traveller?

I stepped in front of the oddcouple and asked if they were both boarding a flight today? Just me the woman replied and she proceeded to act very nervous?. No eye contact?

I asked the man to step aside, took the female out of the snake and away from Bob the builder…asked her some security questions.?

She was too late to board her flight to D.C.. how ever she was not yet aware of this fact?.

I was getting an ear bashing! I must get this flight I have to be back at work in D.C tomorrow! Sorry to inform you I replied, in the first instance you must be at the airport three hours prior to a flight! The gate has closed on the flight you were booked on?

I took the pax to a check in desk and got her a different flight? The lady had now become quite grateful? Sorry I was so rude to you she said but I have had the worst Christmas holiday possible and I have to be back at work tomorrow.

Well you will get back to D.C tomorrow! Just on a later flight I replied, I was about to leave, when the lady asked if I was due a coffee break? I arranged to meet her in Costa's coffee bar in the departure lounge, just as I was leaving I asked if she had met the guy she was with on the internet?

WOW, How did you guess that? She said!

I just smiled at her and said I see this sort of thing a lot at the airports?

I have to go back to work we arranged a time to meet in the departure lounge for the coffee and chat!

Jenny the pax was still amazed how I had sussed the Internet guy out that she had been to London to see?

They had been chatting on Craigs List.?

Jenny was invited to cross the pond.

Cross the pond to spend Christmas and the New Year holidays? In London with Ned! They were both looking for Love.

It was quite apparent that things had not worked out for Ned and Jenny?.

I only had a ten minute coffee break so we exchanged e-mail addresses.

I received an email from Jenny the following day?

Could I possibly help her?

She had arrived back in D.C minus her luggage?

I suggested that she rang the airline etc and if she had no luck to get in touch?

A few days later another e-mail from jenny?, She had no luck with her luggage? She had gone back to Dulles airport to United airlines and there was no trace of her luggage?

Would I check at Heathrow?

I did this and it actually took me quite some time! I had to go to arrivals which was still way busy with the Christmas/New Year rush, queued for ever, finally got the location of Jennie's luggage?

Dulles airport, same day she arrived?

I emailed Jenny and gave her the info!

So how did you get that info and the United people could not find my luggage?

Thank you would be a lot better!

When I had finished explaining.

Security etc?

I still do not think the penny had dropped?

Ok I said, so if you go to Dulles airport and go to Arrivals?

What if I go there and my luggage is not there?

I just told you it is there!

But I went there at the week-end and my luggage was not there.

Trust me it is there!

The luggage was retrieved, Jenny rang me at home to thank me for finding her wordly goods!

Invited me over to D.C as a thank you for finding her baggage!, said she owed me dinner!. Then she proceeded to tell me the story of her visit to Ned in London.?

He was grade "A" ass hole.21ST century Persona male chauvonista.. Ola!

They had met on the internet..

Craigs list!.No less! They emailed and chatted on the telephone, this is usually a good sign if the guy wants to talk to you on the phone? Then decide it would be a good idea for Jenny to "Cross the Pond"

Love Crosses the Pond.com

Chapter Eight

Dulles airport……… Absolutely ….Freezing cold.

Excuse me! Where is the train station located for D.C.

In D.C.!Actually .hmm excuse me!, .I need to catch a train to get into D.C.?

Lady! If you find a train from Dulles airport into D.C. you need to come back and tell ME where it runs from.

Ok…..So there are no trains?…..weird I thought?

The man decided to be a bit more helpful once he realized I worked at the airports in London and what I did?

So helpful that I got V.I.P treatment!

I was passed to one of the guys co-workers, Nancy.

Nancy took me through to arrivals via the workers route. and explained that there was a bus that went into D.C! Gave me the bus number and location of the bay it left from..

Thanks!

Nancy pointed out a ramp that she used. It was quicker and the workers used the ramp to get outside from the airport?

It was quite a drop down onto the street level, down on the sidewalk Nancy ran past me to catch her bus, Bye Ruby, nice meeting you! Likewise I chorused. Oh by the way you have to have the correct change for the bus?

Back in arrivals I found a bank, changed my large dollar note for some change?

The teller wanted to know what change I needed?

Change for the bus?. I had five minutes to catch the next bus!.

Any one know how much change the lady needs for the bus into D.C.

I did a fantastic slide down the ramp The wheels on my suitcase gave me extra speed!

I would deffo pass the audition for the movie

Ice Age Three

I had arranged to meet Jenny at Grand Union station in D.C, did the bus go there?

Please. Say yes?

Nancy had told me the name of a station that I should get off the bus.

China Town?

My fellow passengers decided to assist! A South American guy got out a map about the size of the Washington Post, and explained the Metro.

Another passenger got involved, he agreed with the other passenger …It would be better for me to stay on the bus and get off at Laffeyette?

Then it was two stops to Grand Union station, the first guy said for me to get off the bus at the same time as him and he would show me which metro line to catch? .What a nice guy!

Half the bus was involved with my safe journey into D.C? Keep talking we like your accent?

Ok yah.

I felt like Sandra Bullock? In Speed, ok my hands were not on the wheel, but I was the person of the moment! Lady in distress!

My original stop that I had paid for arrived?

Gallery Place!, China Town? The bus Driver yelled

your stop lady?

I am staying on the bus, Thanks!

You only paid up to here!

Before I could answer the driver! all the passengers on the bus chorused.

The lady is staying on a couple more stops.

The driver was out numbered..

I got the red line metro to Grand Union Station, then met up with Jenny.

She had finished work, we collected her car and drove to her place on Capitol Hill.

Jenny had arranged a busy schedule for the weekend!

Jet lag would have to wait!

Glad rags on, It was freezing! We just had to wear the furs! It was quite a hike from jenny's back to Grand union station.

Jenny in a full length sable, me in a full length silver fox. I Could not wear the coat in London which Jenny found rather odd?.

We caught the metro to Connecticut Avenue, went to The mayflower hotel to have a girly Martini and catch up chat. It was still early evening.

The bar was full of Suits.

I ordered a ginger martini and Jenny had a chocolate martini, we were about to pay when a couple of suits told the barman to charge the drinks to their account it was their pleasure to buy the two beautiful ladies a drink.

We've pulled and it was early evening! Jenny wanted to bring me to the Mayflower hotel to show me where she met her lunchtime internet dates?.

For the past couple of years she had done the whole Internet dating in D.C.

Lunch dates, Dinner dates. Christmas had been her first cross the pond internet date.!

We had a couple of hours to kill before we were to meet up with Neeta and Dee our lady dates at Zorbas, so jenny told me the story of her meeting Ned in London .he had been quite a Cad!

He was a bit of a male chauvinist?

Jenny was quite vocal about it, so they compromised on that and did the sightseeing around London. Jenny was expected to clean house for Ned and take out the trash etc of which she did not do!

Jenny got a flu bug and stayed in bed, Ned left her to her own devices and of course once jenny got over the flu she wanted to go back to D.C. He had not been very kind to her.

Ned was apologetic and asked Jenny to stay longer! She changed her ticket and things got worse? Ned fancied Russian and Ukrainian women, Jenny actually had Ukrainian family history but Ned was actually into dating women from the Eastern Bloc countries?

When they did go out together, Ned would eyeball other women, How nice!

When Jenny met me at London Heathrow airport I was the friendliest caring person she had come across on her trip to London hence me now sitting in he Mayflower hotel on

Conneccticut Ave..Washington D.C. Exchanging our stories on internet dating.

Back out in the cold night air ! we walked to The Spy Lounge.

It was a cool bar! We had more martini's,Rose Petal for me, and a house martini for Jenny. We were taking pictures, Jenny asked a man if he would take our photo? Jenny told the guy. This is my friend Ruby, she works at The London airports and she is on the F.B.I Hit list!

A bit of a conversation stopper! Are you really on the F.B.I hit list Ruby. Well yes but I don't usually advertise that fact. Jenny was embellishing the fact that I was indeed and narrated some of my success stories of catching pax with fake passports etc. you have nice teeth for a European? What! I asked Jenny to explain.

Americans think that most Europeans have bad teeth so he was actually being complimentary to you about your teeth. well I know that Jenny I just did not realize that's how Americans thought of most Europeans. Well you learn something every day.

It was time to go to meet Neeta and Dee over at Zorbas cocktail lounge, the girls were already there when we arrived. More drinks and then we started to swop stories on our Internet dating. Jenny was still upset about her London trip with Ned, the girls could not believe how mean Ned had been to Jenny, the audacity of the man wanting her to clean his apartment and take out the trash and leaving her alone when she was ill. Another date Jenny went on which was a lunch date! She did not really like the guy and once he realized he was not going to see her again he used his cell phone to take a picture of her boobs…cheeky.

Neeta told us about her latest meeting with a guy she met on line. She had given him her cell phone number, a pretty normal thing to do one would imagine!. On meeting up with the guy she realized he was not for her so she was truthful and told him that she did not want to see him again. He got quite nasty about being dumped and wrote her cell phone number in public places so she got a lot of interesting phone calls.

Dee's online beau dumped her at Virginia Beach that was extremely embarrassing! He dumped her in front of his friends, left her at the beach., and no way of getting back to D.C because she had traveled to the beach with him! She got back to DC after a Good Samaritan had seen her upset and he offered her a lift home. The girls were left with the decision that the men had made them feel worthless and they had tried to be honest. They were eager to know my attempts at dating my on line beaus so I told them about Sniff Lauren and Sir Prancelot they could not stop laughing at my scenarios with my dates.

We had played the game and been up front!

"Who" made these men the final judge as our "Worth as women?

Unfortunately we did!.

As Women

We wanted to be perfect dates.

These men did not hold the true measure of our "Worth"

Men!

Did not have the right to take it away from us.

I also added,.Ladies!

You Can dress a pig in a suit!

But you can't stop it grunting!

The men I dated were married men, masquerading as single men!

Our lady pack was getting a lot of attention and some of the men close by to us had over heard our plight with the men we had dated.

You ladies are beautiful women why would those men want to treat you like that?

We had been made to feel bad about ourselves with the treatment our dates had disched out to us. They had been deceitful, and a little cruel.

Chapter Nine

When God created Woman he was working late on the sixth day.

An angel came by and said! Why spend so much time on that one?

And the Lord answered.

“Have you seen all the specifications I have to meet to shape her

She must be washable, but not made of plastic, have more than two hundred moving parts which all must be replaceable and she must function on all kinds of food. She must be able to embrace several kids at the same time, give a hug that can heal anything from a bruised knee to a broken heart and she must do all this with only two hands.

The Angel was impressed.

Just two hands……Impossible!

And this is the standard model?

Too much work for one day…Wait until tomorrow and then complete her.

I will not said the Lord. I am so close to completing this creation which will be

The favorite of my heart.

She cures herself when sick and she can work eighteen hours a day.

The Angel came closer and touched the woman.

But you have made her so soft Lord.

She is soft said the Lord. But I have also made her strong. You can’t imagine what she can endure and overcome.

Can she think the Angel asked?

The Lord answered

Not only can she think, she can reason and negotiate

The Angel touched the woman's cheek.

Lord, it seems this creation is leaking!

You have put too many burdens on her!

She is not leaking

…It’s a tear

What is it for? Asked the Angel

And the Lord said

Tears are her way of expressing grief, her doubts, her love, her loneliness, her suffering and her pride.

This made a big impression on the Angel

Lord you are a genius

You thought of everything. The woman is indeed marvellous!

Indeed she is!

Woman has strengths that amazes man. She can handle trouble and carry heavy burdens.

She holds happiness, love and opinions.

She smiles when feeling like screaming.

She sings when she feels like crying, cries when she is happy and laughs when she is afraid.

She fights for what she believes in.

Stands up against injustice.

She doesn't take no for an answer when she can see a better solution.

She gives herself so her family can thrive. She takes her friend to the doctor if she is afraid.

Her love is unconditional.

She cries when her kids are victorious, she is happy when her friends do well.

She is glad when she hears of a birth or wedding

Her heart is broken when a next of kin or friend dies.

But she finds the strength to get on with life.

She knows that a kiss and a hug can heal a broken heart.

There is only one thing wrong with her.?

SHE FORGETS WHAT SHE IS WORTH!

.

It made sense that we needed to know we had done nothing wrong, We were nice people and should feel good about ourselves. Ok the guys we had dated were not so nice, onwards and forwards there must be some nice men around?

James made his entrance into Zorba's. Jenny had dated James and they were now just friends. I was introduced to James he was so intensely good looking, charming and attentive.

After the introductions more drinks! James and I sat apart from the girls he decided to tell me about one of his internet dates that had quite frankly freaked him out a little.

He had nick named the woman "Mellow Lip kiss"

Mellow Lip kiss had been married, her husband literally dumped her to go and teach English in China and marry a Chinese woman! She decided unbeknown of course to James that she now had to go out and get a replacement husband.

As simple as that! To her.

"What a selfish Woman! "

James had been trawling the inter-net checking his suitable date fishing line!

Mellow lip kiss had advertised herself as Gr8date with a carefully orchestrated profile including professional. Photo shot pictures. Attractive energetic professional seeking Mr. Right..

James arranged to meet mellow in Bajofondo cocktail lounge, she is fashionably late, shows up! ok he said she did look as good as her photo, but there was no chemistry between them, after half an hour of stilted conversation and a couple of over priced martini's. Mellow had done the bio on James, he was a high earner lived in a fashionable district of D.C and he was single available.

Actually James had decided to end the evening!

Mellow had realized that there would not be a return date with James. She decided to wrestle with James tongue.

She realized that she had to get his attention! Decided to slide her hand inside his open necked shirt, slide her hand down to the family heirlooms!

The following morning! James wakes up next to mellow, it's the weekend so no rush to work.!

They went for a bicycle ride, James used her ex husbands cycle. Mellow wanted James to stay over the weekend and meet her parents?

There was a family gathering!

Most of the conversation at this gathering was about how nice mellows ex husband was!

Ghost photos of Mellows husband were strategically placed around the house.

The family talked over James and basically ignored him.

James decided it was time to leave both the family gathering and mellow too!

Mellow had other plans and asked James to stay over.

Being the Gentleman he was he decided to stay!

"So" he would lie back and enjoy the fun!.

……………..Maybe…………………………

Whoooooooooooo.

After the family members left, an ex boyfriend of Mellows turned up on the doorstep!

James went home, enough was enough.

Mellow had other plans?

She turned up on James door step later that evening, she wanted to parle about James moving in with her, she made a perfect O with her left index finger! Then pointed her right index finger through the O. Know what I mean?

"Do you think we could date for a while first ? James suggested".

Kinda you know get to know each other first?

He said he was busy at the moment and would call Mellow later.

He did not phone her!. Mellow rang James asked why he had not phoned?

She became obsessive. Demanding to know why he had not phoned her? She said he was pulling away from her. Mellow asked James to come over and stay with her. He made polite noises about working the following day, then Mellow started to blaspheme which is when James decided to end the phone call….click to the crazy chick.

Hey dude what's with the surveillane?

James had gone to his neighbors pad "Catbird and Craigster's. We spotted a blue Saturn outside your pad over a week ago? Turns up every night and stays for the whole night! Who do you think it is dude?

Probably some crack head James replied.

The fact remains there is a stranger in our neighborhood catbird replied, Craigster and I are committed to deterring him.

Catbird raised both arms and made the universal gesture of a man loading a shotgun and aiming it.

Your not going to shoot him James asked in astonishment!

Nah

"No night scope".

Catbird and Craigster are roommates. They are perfect neighbors to James and are worried about the blue Saturn that had been parking all night for over a week outside James apartment. They were normal hard working guys, ambitious generous to a fault, don't drink alcohol, smoke or swear!, .But beneath their patina of American wholesomeness lies a dark secret?.

They are weekend warriors Their condo stores enough weapons stashed in it to overthrow a small African nation. Hey James do you want to join us on the WATCH! We've got extra night scopes, the scopes will light the car up with freaky green light, and he won't be able to scratch his ass without us knowing! Should be cool. I will have to pass on the offer tonight, I have a hot date with my cot! The crazy chick is phoning me at all hours so it is dreamland for me tonight.

It's two am. Someone is knocking at my door? James scrambles to open the door! Mellow is standing there demanding to know why James won't commit to her?

She needed to know if? It was over.?

James

Showing up at two am is a bit intense and stalkerish!

Mellow

I need answers.

James

And I need some sleep.

Mellow brushed past James and plops her tearful body on his couch.

Lets talk.

James

I need some sleep

Mellow

Fuck you asshole

James

Say good night to the bad man

Mellow

User

James shows mellow the door.

A moment later there is a commotion on the street outside the apartment. The cops are out front and they are talking to Mellow. James goes out front and asks to no one in particular.

What happened.

Mellow replied "Honey I was getting in my car when they pulled me up" she snuggled up to James as if nothing happened.?

Tell them everything is all right will you Sweetie pie.

One of the officers comes over holding mellow,s license.

I've got bad news for you miss, we're impounding your car.

Why

You have over five hundred dollars in unpaid parking tickets says the officer!

Mellow looks at James and demands

Do something! you work for the government!

James looked at the car ! Catbird and Craigsters conversation reminded him that the car was the.

Blue Saturn.

James looked over to Catbird and Craigsters darkened apartment windows, and the green glint of a night scope.

His hero's

The tow truck winches Mellow's car up and away.

Mellow was sreaming at James! Do something I have to go to the airport to collect Donnie?

Oh yes the ex boyfriend James replied.

James went back inside his apartment and closed the door on a back ground tirade of Mellow screaming .

Bastard, User.

Said mentally to himself, good bye to what could have been a very nasty relationship and said a mental thank you to his hero's of the night watch.

Catbird and Craigster.

CHAPTER TEN

5)

The girls and myself are congregated at Mei n' yu in Georgetown a funky happening DC. cocktail bar and eatery.

We were just there as a meeting point and to have a couple of warm up Martini's before moving on to the "Rhino bar"

we ended up staying longer than anticipated.

Ok Ya

"A group of bachelors" Who knows? Would we actually ever know?

Were vying for our attention, they were fun but quite cheeky chaps. Their spokesman came over and handed business cards to us!. We over heard you ladies are moving on to the Rhino bar, we have a dinner reservation here at Mei n' yu.

We would love to join you at the Rhino bar! later. He stuck the cards down Jennie's ample cleavage.

That moved us.

Rapido!

Out in the freezing night air we decided to give the "Rhino a miss"

Ok Yah!

Hailed a cab and headed back to China Town.

We had arranged to meet James after dinner at the "Spy Lounge" he wanted to continue the conversation about his internet dating experiences.

James did arrive

Because it was a girly night out.

We re arranged our conversation on his inter-net dating over a brunch chow pow, wow!.

The following lunch time!

Sunday brunch!

Blues alley.

The venue was cool,

The conversation was even cooler.

Whoo hoo.

Jenny and I were brunching with the girls ,

James and I sat just out of earshot, close enough to be part of the group. And important!

After "Mellow" I did not think James would have another control freak inter-net date?

Well! James said I decided to go on a

Professional Business dating site

Thought it would be safe?

I assumed protocol would be in there somewhere on the 21st dating for middle class DC. Professionals.

The luck James had been having he decided to go for the lawyer lady who had advertised her self in a business like manner. Nice professional photo! A bit gothic tho?

They met up for a drink at Psychedelic Gothic

Live and let live

…whooooo…..Hooooooooo

Ok James said Lawyer lady was a little different! Dressed in gothic black, including her make up! But he knew she was by day.

A Lawyer

They got on well… decided to consummate their date! Back at her place!.

" We named her "Wicca".

After all she is a lawyer.

.

James?

Question

"Roofies"

you spiked my drink with roofies?

Well I sort of passed out James mentioned to Wicca.

"You know like the morning after the night before"

After our hot date, staying over at your place after we consummated our first date!.

Work was deffo in the equation, it was a mid week date.

Did you by the remotest chance spike my drink with a you know? Like a flunitrazepam,or similar molecularly chained benzodiazepine derivative that could possibly have the following side effects.

Slurred speech.

Loss of motor control.

Drowsiness.

Amnesia.

You mean roofies?

Did I put roofies in your drink?

Is that what you are asking me James?

James laughs and states

Admission is the first step to recovery.

He promised he would not have her thrown in jail!

James is still so up for another hot date with Wicca..

She has a fantasy?

As most women do!.

Pray tell?

Wicca has a desire to be raped.

And so the story goes.

Step into "Wicca fantasy land".

Her sick twisted fantasy was

To be raped!

"Ye gads. A woman's worst nightmare is the possibility of being raped at some point in her life!"

So this twisted lawyer lady that! at some point in her career would be representing a rape victim. Actually has a strong desire to be raped per se! for her solo twisted fantasy!

So her story is to be portrayed something like?

"A story line "

She was an African girl living in the bush! Dressed in a leopard skin bikini her brothers had decided to tie her to a tree!

James had to dress himself up in a Giraffe costume? Pretend that he had stumbled across this young girl tied to a tree, He would be the frisky giraffe that came across this vision………. And rape her.

James had to get in the

Giraffe mode

as in costume!

This thing smells and hey honey do you really think that a giraffe would rape a woman?… By the way this costume

What is it made from? Dish cloths!

Orange terry towel dish cloths.

Yeh James replied I did not think that Fredericks of Hollywood supplied Giraffe rape costumes.

James put his hands on his hips, Well his hooves! On his haunches!

Just get into the mood and go along with my fantasy Wicca demands.

I draw the line when I have to dress up like a fucking giraffe to get you horny James retorts.!

I just can't get into the character!

Another whacked emotional vulture looking for a carcass to pick James had by now realised. Crazy emotional, unstable people do that sort of thing. It gives them a sense of purpose to their ..hmmm otherwise psychotic lives. Nameley control freaks .arrggg……

A crazed goth lawyer!

Where is Christian Carter when you need him?

Time to go back to the inter-net date fishing line.

Plentyoffish.com

A happening new date site which is a free site and very popular amongst the cool 21s[t] century internet dating scene.

Praise be to Marcu Frind Ceo of plentyoffish.com

After that riveting story! as non fiction as it was! James and I moved closer to our friends group and enjoyed the ambience that Blues Alley had to offer, and had some fun drinks with our cross the pond friends.

I quietly suggested to James that maybe some

P2p networking was the order of the day!

Peer to peer networks are!

Online communities where members share, search and download files which are located on their personal computers.

They share their personal files, download music and movie files are commonly shared in p2p networks.

There is no central computer where files are stored!

It is an upgrade from ims and not as intrusive as instant messaging. Instant messaging can form deception from salient characteristics that abusers form. They create certain parameters of a personality. That they create to form soley to entice you into their whacky world!.

The boogy men live on these sites usually msn and hot mail…The Nigerian and Russian scammers use these sites so watch out! They post false photos so you do not know they are Nigerian…or Russian! They are so desperate to achieve UK or US residence .Ok they use the free sites. The sites give you the chance to report these scammers!

Delete them.

CHAPTER ELEVEN.

Netiquette!

There are no set rules per se!

The phenomenal growth of online dating and the number of people from all age groups and persuasions use them as their primary source for meeting people and looking for "THE ONE"

Anonyminity

On the net you do not have to give your real name! If You choose to.

It is solely at your discression! What you do need to be aware of is the fact that the abusers on the web do have multi user names and the hardened abusers swing both ways? create female names …...vice versa .

Scarey stuff, .but unfortunately the case!

Do not be put off by the abusers

There are some nice people to be met on the net.

Boo……

Lol……

Usually decent guys that pay a fee to join a hopefully reputable site have probably exhausted all the free sites and realize hey pay a fee it is safe.

Is it?

MarcusFrind may not agree!

I must admit some of the nicest people I have met have come from Marcus's site.

www.plentyoffish.com

On the positive side ..Is there anything but to have a positive attitude? Refreshingly a few new free sites are out there and ok the waccos appear on them but I'm sure the seasoned users know how to avoid them like the plague

Ok the pig is out there in his suit.grunting….just gagg him.

Go to the cool happening free sites and have some fun.

A couple of free sites I am happy to recommend are

Craigs list.

Plentyoffish.com

Sugardaddie.com

Seeking millionaire.com

There are no set rules per se on netiquette dating or friendship!. Just use your common sense. There are lots of players out there on the net, play them at their own game and never put all your eggs in one basket!. The players are egotistical people with many beaus.

Living in your home of bricks and mortar would not normally give you any chance of finding a suitor!But hey! hit the keyboard and surf the world .it's very exciting. There are people of many persuasions looking for friendship also maybe hoping to meet the one!

Go on…..You know you want to.

CHAPTER TWELVE

Ok James had bared his souls so justifiably it was my turn to lighten his load.

And the girls were all ears on my foolish moment.

I had decided to go .International dating! Thought it may be safer!

The site I used was free for women, because the men paid! numb nut mois thought I would be safe and of course the site does say if you come across abusers on the site to report them……..watch this space…

A crime scene investigator no less so .one can imagine that I felt pretty safe.

We corresponded and to cut to the chase I was visiting Florida where this Player was living…..three months later. He did not want to wait to see me three months down the line so after many e-mails and phone calls. very romantic, honey would you come and visit me sooner if I pay for your ticket from England? I had the time to do this but another trans atlantic flight a few months before my holiday was not in my budget!

I agreed and searched for flights. Player said ok book the flight and as you are coming back to the States on vacation I will give you the $$$$ when you arrive saves me using western union for a fat fee and you will not have to pay exchange rates! I am talking to a police man…Ok…..yah!

I book the flight! The prior evening to my flight I stay at my daughter and son in laws house have dinner and drinks, .in the holiday mode. Bit of karaoke too! Woo.Hoo!

Because we had over indulged on the wine and song I forgot to set my alarm call! Oh oh!

I was shaken awake by my daughter…you will have to move it to get to gatwick airport the London traffic is really bumper to bumper now, and it is absolutely monsoon raining.

I was up and out driving onto the M3 within twenty minutes. The traffic by now was moving so slow because of the time and the rain. The rain was coming down in torrents! The windshield wipers were at the fastest speed possible! I was lane hopping like a road hog and thankfully made it to the airport within the allowed time before the flight closed! Parked my car at the outside perimeter parking

I self checked in then went to bag drop my case got my boarding pass then realized I had left my cell phone in my car! I needed the phone to call my new man ….his phone number and details were in my phone. I still had time to go back to the out side parking, so I jumped on the car parking bus then…you just know don't ya with so far two things already gone wrong there just has to be a third? things always happen in threes. Some one on the other side was warning me that this meeting was not meant to be?

I got off at the bus stop where I thought I had got on, started to walk to the row of parked cars that I had memorised the number of where I had parked my car?! Then the heavens opened, .the monsoon rain was back! I retrieved the phone from the car after calling myself all the idiots and dumb blonde names I could. Saw the bus heading way over at the bus stop so I part ran slipped and slided to see the driver pulling away minus mois. Waited twelve minutes for the next bus to arrive….It said so on the bus stop! My clothes were soaking wet, .My hair was plastered to my head, the hang over head!....Other passengers were arriving at the bus stop in their dry clean clothes. Oh the rain had magically stopped...I looked like something that had crept out of the lake! .my eye make up had run. very goulishly......no bus it took twenty minutes to arrive and I was starting to panic I go back to the terminal and go through security. I.was asked the mandatory questions about liquids etc do you have any mascara madam?.I thought the guy was being flippant.! Oh yes I replied halfway down my face!.......What make up I did have in my bag was sacred and necessary for repairs and I was keeping it!

I got through passport control and headed for the loo, my boarding gate was a fifteen minute walk and the flight was announced. I dried my hair under the hand drier which lasted for about two minutes then desperately tried to control my now chemically producted nutty professor hair style....whoo hoo!

So those products do actuallly work? my long sleek blonde hair which I had painstakingly pampered the previous evening, With generous amounts of products promising to keep my hair looking groomed, sleek and with extra firm hold! Certainly had a firm hold on my hair folicles.

I boarded the aircraft, and once we were airborn headed for the loo again to repair my make up and swoop my crispy hair into a pony tail a la pineapple style.Lovely! I am not sure who was laughing the loudest James or the girls? they were firing all sorts of questions at me between stifled giggles.

So I land in Orlando and go through the usual sequences of arriving in a foreign land...Head to the carousel to collect my suitcase and once I have my case head for the loo again this time to seriously sort out my hair. I found my portable hair straightness ! then did some magic with those!. My cell phone rang it was my daughter louise, checking I had arrived ok. I narrated my tale of woe and she was absolutely in fits of laughter.....I had phoned player and he was running late thank goodness! He kept saying that I had to sit on a bench outside arrivals? Bit cheeky I thought but hey ho?.

I waited as instructed on the bench outside arrivals from BA. Cars kept kerb crawling....Mainly because of security it was just a set down area! Then the girls kept ringing me to see if player had collected me! Not yet I half hoped ,I said I had plan B to fall back on which was at this precise time and moment more appealing! Player turned up! He was a little bit like his photo but a lot shorter, I wanted to ask where the rest of his legs were! Then I remembered all his photo's were of him sitting down? Hmmm, oh oh.

Ok now James and the girls were starting to give their input! The questions were more or less what I had already asked myself?

So why did he not be a gentleman and meet me at the arrivals

Doahhhh...so he could drive away from me if he did not like what he saw!

I imagine?

So he did not drive away! Our journey to players house was about an hour and a half. player decided to stop at a restaurant en route which gave us time to chill and catch up. I must admit I got the impression that he was looking for a fling and not as described in his profile from the dating site...Searching for a long term relationship?

At our rendezvous, "His home" I was introduced to his dog! It was made crystal clear that the dog was very important and was treated like a human…Really.

No ghost photos of his supposed ex wife? She was Russian, hmmm I was beginning to get the picture Player had bought a Russian bride! He did not admit that so either she was back in Russia on vacation and that explained why player was so insistent on me being in the US at the precise time he wanted me to be there and not three months later? Well I was here and plan B could still be put into operation.

I rang my friend plan b. she lived in the same town to make arrangements for a meet. We arranged to meet at Captain Hirams ,so I relayed the message to player. I do not drink alcohol, really? .Oh oh "you said that you did? Ok cancel that meet Rose" I was now whispering down the phone, Rosie he does not drink alcohol, and he smokes . Yak poo, he said he did not smoke cigarettes and he does. Ok I will come and collect you! get your stuff together, ok no probs. Player was busy talking to his dog calling her sweetheart and saying how gorgeous she was? He went out for a walk with his beloved dog! Well he carried the dog so her paws would not hurt, said he would be about twenty minutes. Rose arrived and collected me……Well he would have dumped me at the airport if he did not like me…I was dumping him at his home and he deserved dumping for telling so many lies……My mother told me when I was young! trust a policeman I guess the passage of time changes a lot of things!

James and the girls agreed that they would have done the same thing!

Ok yah.

So we all had more drinks. Once the questions had stopped. Ok so I do blonde very well I stated! Our group was now in side-splitting laughter at my total expense.! So I decided to go for the lose your breath type laughter that my next story .I just knew would leave them breathless!. I narrate my story, .totally non-fiction stuff!

Large brandy in hand. All eyes and ears are mine for this latest faux paux. I think I have achieved a larger audience. My drinks are being bought by a few by standers eagerly waiting after drying their wet tears of laughter For the next story. I am being passed business cards and offers of a weekly story corner in the venue.

So!I begin!

I left the suitable date fishing line company, sorry Marcus.

Cruising along on

www.kisscafe

A site very close to Marcu's a neighboring Canadian Vancouver free dating run by Angelo! portrays himself as a dog… A loud chorus of Nahhhhhh He he hee's are quite loud now Sorry Angelo! .Don't believe mois?.Take a look guys … The guys are now wild eyed and looking at me as if ………..

So my details are on there for the world to see…

After my dismal failures on inter-net man meetings, I receive a few

Mwaaa's from kiss café. ohhhhh La La.

Some interesting profiles of men that wish to chat to me.

I how ever have decided that, ok I am half heartedly doing this. But there is one guy that keeps contacting me. I weaken uh ohhhh, My blonde moment is out there big time. Ok cut me some slack! Guys! I may be had one too many glasses of vino.

This ere guy just loved my profile, hmmm

What this guy liked was the fact that I am a Brit and he was so desperate for UK residency. His charm was in full Love you long time mode!

My scammer radar was not awake.

I had been working long hours at my job. Golf season was in full swing and lots of events were happening for large numbers of societies!

I got home! knackered .in need of a decent libation. Mainly To sustain myself and retain a hopefully believing that I was Living la vida dolce moment before returning to work the following day at a totally unsociable early hour. Do golfers ever sleep? Suffering sleep depravation…I decide to have myself a sociable surf on the

Kisscafe site. Glass of working mans champagne in hand, Cava!

You have six messages? Three mwaha's and a personal invite?

All from the same guy we shall name him.

SCAMMER!

The guys are now .giving me the oh, oh's.

The photo's. The charm, my scam radar is still asleep.

Intoxicated with Senor Cava, and all the charm. This guys carefully orchestrated script! I gave him my cell phone number after mucho requests!

Then whils't I waited for his call quickly checked out his profile again, Said he was Philippine from Manila. 45 wants children!

Whoops I realized too late. The call arrived, I was now compus mentos.

I made stilted conversation with the guy! I now knew he was a scammer. I questioned the fact. So you are in Nigeria? Yes I am working on a contract there. Really I say, actually you sound Nigerian too what are you a chameleon, What you saying woman's? well my sister-in law just happens to be Philippine so what I am saying to you is, factually I know the Philippine dialect! Lots of Nigerian chat in the backgound! Well look I really have to go I want you for my woman's…I have a question for you?

WILL YOU MARRY ME!

WELL I KNOW WE ARE ON ANGELOS SITE ……….BUT THIS GUY IS BARKING MAD.HEY NO HE IS A DESPERADO SCAMMER.NIGERIAN NO LESS…

So desperate for uk residency, Probably all the back gound nigerian voices I can hear is the headquarters for the big boss scammers. I let the guy I know he is a faker but he now becomes so.

Prince Charming.

Probably his bosses are directing him .He passes the phone to a friend of his. A deep Nigerian voice is saying my friend loves you! He wants to marry you. Fuck you mad men scammers is my response!

I click end conversation and put a teat on the brandy bottle.for my wake up call. "I decided an affair with Monseur courvoisier would! ok leave me a bit stupid, but I could always leave him alone until I needed him again. At least he departed at the base of a glass!

If I say scammer bombarded me with MSN messages, It would be an understatement. My cell phone was constantly ringing with his calls…..A message on kisscafe e-mail header read

I need you in my life!…………

When I went on line his constant interruptions via msn were so intrusive.. As much as ignored him .for a whole day. So at the end of my tether I answered his 1ooth message.

Scammer………Oh baby where have u been!

Avoiding you…

I need you in my life. Will you come to Nigeria now? Get on a plane and come to Nigeria..

Muse was in giggle mode in my head! wearing a big hat humming the wedding march!

Mois..

Look I know you are a scammer, so .leave me alone

Scammer

What you say woman's

Mois

Errrr…leave me alone……factually you are a scammer…….just go and leave me alone.

Scammer

Common woman's

Mois

Attaining my dignity. Common is rude, maybe I ruffled your feathers or head dress by dissing you! Just understand! I know you are a scammer. Tell your bosses, not this blonde ok!. What tribe are you from? .ok guys I was now a little bit .pissed off!

Another man supposedly from the U.S had been sending me a few Mwa's and messages on www.kisscafe, so I eventually returned a poilite thank you and then he asked for my msn name.

Did you they all chorused?

Nooo mmm, no err…actually

Yes.

This guy chatted about how nice he thought I was etc …He was working away from home? My muse was whispering in my ear, do not trust him. I was the type of girl he would like to marry? mm , so I said to the guy ha working away from home? home being the US. Yes he said I live in America.

I suppose you are working in Nigeria then?. How did you know that? He said. Well I can tell by your grammar?

It was the very same man that I had been scammed by. He was using a different photo!

Attempt number three by the very same man was to imitate a

US soldier.

With a photo dressed in military uniform of a united states trooper, with a united states flag in the background!

A very cute message for me ..actually lots of cute messages!

James and the girls were so obviously distressed at this information! The scammer was sick to use a photo of a us soldier.

Attempt number four by the same scammer.

A highly decorated major in the us army.

Photo of him in full army dress uniform with all his medals. In the background of the photo an American flag.

My messages were getting cuter, infect on the first message from him I got a WOW…

Another message was he was looking for a bride?

Ding a ling!

He lived in Alaska?

He lived in Nigeria.

It was the same guy using a different image.

Scary stuff.

Who were the people from the other images that scammer was using?

How dare these people pray on decent individuals?

I mean where is the safety net…

These scammers are allowed to cruise the internet.

There is no safety net!

Scarey heh? They were amazed at my story. I actually had another story. Thought I would leave it for the moment. There was not a dry eye in the house! Lots of laughter at my expense, But we were all friends.

Cross the pond friends. Lots of love in the room! "Genuine ok"

Ok!

They wanted a finale!

Ok ..I sort of had two stories to tell!

One was a favorite of mine , and not a bad story!

It was a very special story!

Ok ..the one that was the favorite of my heart was indeed a definite cross the pond love story…….

It happened so!…

We are amongst friends, friends are for sharing special moments with?

I had the attention of the room.

I had made a lot of friends.

I met my special beau on

www.datingdirect.com

he had paid a fee to join this site to meet a special woman!

My info was on this site so as a female I did not pay,how ever they had all my info for their database. And hey! I got a response from? ok Canada .Vancouver no less.

The guy claimed to be Swiss.

We corresponded.

Special man was infect of German decent, ok he had been brought up in Switzerland for a huge part of his life.

Moved to Canada in his early yearsas a single guy, bit of a moving heart story going on here so… sorry this part is special and remaining private!

Ok so he meets the love of his life, .marries has two children.

Usual crap stuff! Happens.

He gets divorced!

I have them all still wet eyed! So! I cut to the chase! .well I try to! They now want all the details.

Oh..Canada, Lions and tigers and bears, Mounties.

You live in the uk!, .Buckingham Palace, Queens, Prince's, Princesse's

How romantic………

Well! I continued with my narration!

Special and I exhausted every avenue to be in touch!through initially Dating direct

They would not allow personal email info to be allowed from special, even though he had paid his money? So we used a code to get our personal email addresses to be made available!

We also managed to get our telephone numbers to each other.

Initially this was how we got to know each other Better!

Through talking on the phone at all hours!

He said I was like a drug!………

Loved my accent, . and sense of humor!

Special actually introduced me to?

www.plentyoffish.com

That was how we managed to correspond for nada……Free

We also talked a lot on the phone! At designated times.

Special even gave me telephone wake up calls for work when I had to be for work extra early………

The time zones allowed this!

We became very close!

He was going to Europe in September.

Would I meet him in Europe?

Special was crossing the pond for love!

Would I meet him?

He knew I was a little nervous about a realtionship!

I had been on my own, single for eight years. I had only just started dating again after eight years of being a singleton. My dates from the inter-net sites had produced married men. masquerading as single men!

So he named me his little nun!

Special also went to the trouble of consulting a psychiatrist, He needed to know how to treat a lady that had been single for so long?

CHAPTER THIRTEEN

Bremen Germany.

I am at the airport! My special man who has flown to Gemany from Canada Is in arrivals waiting to greet me.

A few oh's and ah's from my audience!

Wow!............you both actually met up!

Yep he crossed the pond to meet me!

Special; was an international.Tennis player.

He had already flown into Germany..

Frankfurt, played a tennis tournament. Then gone to Switzerland to see family?

Got onto a train to Bremen Germany which was his home town where he was born, he wanted to meet me there to show me his beginnings and just to show me his roots etc.

A few wows and how beautiful were thrown in for good measure from my ever increasing friends now!

So I am at arrivals and there he was.

Special had gone to an awful lot of trouble to make our meeting very memorable...

He had just been on a three hour train trip from Switzerland to come and meet me at Bremen airport!

Arranged a romantic hotel,.actually a boat hotel.I did not know this! He had booked the boat, a two berth luxury vessel berthed in Bremen harbour!

From meeting me at the airport until we left each other two days later!. It was like a fairytale romance!.

Special spoilt me with good man manners! I mean the works.

Mwahhhh.

I was

Wined,candle lit dined , spoilt!........Shown around his home town, boat tours, bus tours, we walked for miles doing all the tourist sights! Talking about each other. Romancing, acting stupid, silly stuff. we did it all!

"We also did the cemetary tour"

Both of specials parents had died when he was in Canada .This was the first time he had been able to visit his parents graves!

Close. To say we got close is an understatement!

Leaving each other was not easy. we had already discussed the fact that .special would like me to visit him in Canada? For now, The moment he was in Europe He had to return to Switzerland to a tennis tournament. could he visit me in the UK the following week-end?

It was a fairytale romance…………..

I had never been treated like a princess before…………….

.

Windsor………..Close to the castle..

The queens castle!

Oackley Manor hotel………..A fitting residence for my new beau…

He had spoilt me in Bremen, The spoiling was to be continued here in the UK

Similar sights were available tourist wise!

.How ever, Special.had a chest infection.. Actually .actually an acute case of Asthma?

Brought on by a couple of cats who were resident in the home of.

The lady, the cats and her daughter where he was a guest.In Switzerland!?

When I left "Special" in Bremen I gave him a cell phone with enough credit on so he could make calls in Europe and be able to stay in contact with me .His cell phone did not have this function!

We went to a pharmacy to get some over the counter medication!

We had planned to walk around Windsor then over the bridge into Eton. The general idea was to see all that Windsor and Eton had to offer all in one day. The following day, Sunday we were going to visit my family for drinks and dinner!

The asthma was quite bad so! .as it was raining I said I would drive the route that the tour bus usually took around Windsor and the Eton tour we could walk after the drive tour.

We did all the touristy stuff, then went to a garage to get some fuel. Special actually decided to check some other stuff in my engine for me..How sweet of him.

He had spotted a pub that he wanted to go to for Dinner that evening

On the outskirts of Windsor.

He said I lived close enough to the pub that if I chose to I could go back and reminisce about our evening there once he was back in Canada.

The following evening we have dinner at my daughter and son-in laws house along with my other daughter!

It was an eventful evening! Quite memorable. Infect.Special was a bit too much?

He was naturally a very outspoken person, bordering on rude. But managed to sweet talk his outspokenness with a con man experience!

I decided to cut the evening short.. we returned to Windsor we had to leave very early the following morning ! I was driving to stanstead airport. Special was flying back to Frankfurt to catch his flight back to Canada.

At Stanstead we talked about me going to Canada in the next couple of months?

Him back in Canada me in the UK. We continued our affair of the heart via web cam and phone calls, he had started to be a bit too much. Me, me, me .Allways bigging himself up!

Said I would never find any man as good looking as him? really?…………"Theres a bit of a challenge"

He was always commenting about money!, He could give me his bank account details. Said he was looking for a RICH WOMAN?

I suggested he searched on www.seekingmillionaire.com

The constant me, me, me was getting tedious. When the time came around for my visit to Canada, I said that I could not get the time off work so would re-arrange the date to visit Vancouver!

I know? I am such a wimp.

I did not contact Player as I had now re-named him. Special was to be remembered from our meeting in Bremen, Germany.

Player was happy surfing along on.

www.plentyoffish.com

we did chat occasionally! He was still bigging himself up,saying lots of women were contacting him from the p.o.f site.

Actually talking of contact? I received a phone call on my cell phone a lady was asking for you? As it was one am in the morning and the call had woken me up, I was a little slow. The woman was asking for you..were you there? I said no! .who is this?. I am his girlfriend from Switzerland? bit cheeky phoning me On my own cell phone I thought. I just said no you were in Canada and I said I am sure you have his contact number there!

Player was a bit lost for words. Unusual for him! In the couple of seconds of silence He came up with a story that the girl was not his girl friend. He was a guest at the house where the girl lived with her mother, actually it was the mother that fancied him

And? I replied have you found your rich blue rinse lady yet? Player worked as a tour guide and literally had the gift of the gabb!

Player had a request for me?

Would I be his guest at his works Christmas party? Plus it was his birthday during the same week at the beginning of December.!

He wanted me to be his guest too at his birthday dinner, he also would like to introduce me to his friends.

How could I say no?

….

CHAPTER FOURTEEN

Air Canada flight to Vancouver! "I had decided that ok! I was beginning to understand that Player was just that! a player. It was nice of him to ask me to be his guest at his works Christmas function so no harm done"?

On my journey I am sat next to an elderly gentleman. He snoozed for most of the flight. When he woke up he started some conversation about my journey to Vancouver….Had I been there before? I said not to Vancouver, but I had been to Canada on many occasions when I was a flight attendant!

Jim my flight neighbor said that he had crossed the pond from Canada to England to visit his girl friend! Said he was eighty one, and he gave a little giggle. Ok I just do hugging now.

He then explained about his girl friend who was also eighty one years young! how they met?

They actually first met when they were both eighteen years,old InYorkshire England during the second world war. Jim was in the Royal Air Force. A trainer pilot .He was seconded to foreign shores. They both promised to keep in touch. War being war they lost touch With each other! They both married different partners. sxty three years later, Jim became a widower. He decided to trace his first love through the friends re-united. Jim said imagine my delight when I actually managed to trace her! .Pat's husband had also died, they decided to meet up in England and were now a couple, Pat was coming over to Canada in the next month to stay.so they could pretend to be eighteen all over again. " The reverse of eighty one"

I wished them all the luck in the world at actually finding each other again.

When we arrived at Vancouver Jim was my escort to the carousel for my baggage and then to the meeting point he was such a gent.

Player was actually working and the arrival time of my flight was in rush hour traffic so we had arranged to meet in downtown Vancouver at a designated bus stop,Player was waiting for me and we caught up on the missing months we had been apart!

He was still bigging himself up so I just played it cool!He mentioned lots of plans for sight seeing!.being a tour guide he was going to be my personal tour guide! Also an old lady friend that he visited occasionally would like me to go to lunch with her? No probs said I would be delighted to go to lunch with his old lady friend.

Arriving at Players apartment. I was given wardrobe space and spent a few minutes unpacking. There were a few lady things in the wardrobe? plus electric curlers! and women sized slippers which cancelled out the thought that may be Player had a feminine side?

I decided to just leave the feminine belongings find in my thoughts?,How ever I decided to be careful with my emotions!

We went out for a short tour of West Vancouver, then had Dinner and catch up chat.

Jet lag caught up, so we decided an early evening and the following day a tour of Vancouver which was cut short by a snow storm, so we went to the cinema then back to the apartment. We were snowed in for a couple of days but managed to go out for long walks in between the snowstorms.

Monday morning Player had to go to work, I was meeting up with his old lady friend for lunch and player was collecting me in the evening from her house. Our lunch trip was quite interesting. Upon meeting Gia I realized she was European old? She did not look her age shall we say, she was not what I was expecting.. The way player had described this infirm old lady I thought may be I needed a medic close by.

Not so!

Bad, bad, player.?

Gia was just as surprised by me and clearly wanted info from me?

It became crystal clear in the first few minutes of our meeting that player was playing with our emotions.

So

You must be very special Ruby! You are only the second woman that has stayed at Players apartment! Well maybe the third woman, but certainly no more I met the first lady she was from Switzerland?

Ding a ling my muse was reminding me of the early hours phone call from a lady in Switzerland? saying she was player's girlfriend! His Canadian girlfriend lives a couple of hours drive from West Vancouver, I have not met her yet! Gila offered the info and I responded with a Spanish shrug. That makes two of us then I said!

So I believe Player is spoiling you Ruby? Cooking dinner for you most nights and giving you a guided tour of Vancouver. Er well actually yes! He is spoiling me somewhat. I realized that Gia was more than just a friend!

He has never cooked for me?

Whoops.

I was spending the next four hours with Gia, and it was fair judgement to say she was a bit ticked off!

It wont' work?, You and Player!I already told him.

Yep! Gia was deffo ticked off!

I decided to put Gia at ease, Look I know Player has lots of girlfriends so trust me I am here by invitation to go to his works Christmas party and his birthday Dinner. With that thought in mind shall we go shopping. I need to get a prezzie for his birthday.

We both now knew our places, so we shopped and bought a birthday gift for player! Then had some lunch, and back to Gia's place to wait for Player to collect me.

Driving back to players apartment he announced that he was expecting a girl to visit him the following week. He had met her on the pof site, she was flying to Vancouver from Scotland.

I said busy you! What about your Canadian girlfriend?

I got the usual what has Gia been saying to you? In her absent defence "I said, she has said nothing. I am just surmising you have a Canadian girlfriend. Swiss girlfriend too player announced!.Oh so the phone call from the Swiss lady that woke me up was infect your girlfriend?

I said to player that he had to understand that things between us were different now! I would always remember Bremen and our special time together there. However right here and now we would only be just friends "Nothing more"

We had by now arrived back at Players apartment. He was clearly not used to being put in his place. He was quite upset at my statement, said he had tears in the back of his eyes…Crocodile tears!

I offered to go to a hotel…Player insisted I stay with him and he was a gent okay things were a little strange now. The birthday party came around and his friends were very nice infect quite sociable to me.

Player behaved like a moron saying he had a different girlfriend every year at his birthday, and the next girl coming to visit him was from Berlin. I could not be bothered to say .thought it was Scotland! However his friends were not so pleased with his behavior, They were asking if I was returning to Vancouver and could they have my e-mail address! Player was amazed. This has never happened before my friends want to stay in touch with you?

I was returning to Blighty in the morning and could not wait to leave!

Once again I promised myself to be extra careful who I met on the dating sites!

.

Chapter fifteen

Ok over the years sites have had to change their status.

To pay to a dating site years ago was politically correct N'cest pas!

I did years ago agree! We had no other choice until Marcus . God bless his soul !and Craigs list appeared. .Many people were pray to the corruption of the sites management.

"I no longer agree that you have to pay!to be actually controlled by a company that you, hmmm actually pay money to join and then they will decide who you can or can not speak to? This is .after you paying a hefty fee to be able to .as you think be allowed to contact a decent person.Actually the premier members? Whoaa, If you like them and want to contact them. You have to pay more money to be allowed access to them? Err hello……

Is it about romance or Mone?……We already paid the money when we joined? So? We have to pay more money?

Make your minds up paying dating sites

Ok Guys put up and shut up you paying sites had your fun and controlling actions for far too long!

The free sites now rule!

Why

No controlling involved?

The free sites make their money from advertising. Usually other dating sites and companies involved with romance.They have all your money to be able to pay to advertise their site?

The free sites at least do have a heart!, they give free advice on how to avoid the scammers. Allow you to report abuse and how to block

Pure bad people!

The free sites make lots of money from advertising. They just need you on their data base!

You are in control…Totally!

If you want to give a guy/gal your e-mail addy or telephone number.

Just do it .The ball is actually in your court.

No you do not have to get out your credit card to do this Marcus has made it possible to be your own boss and chat for free. Talk to whom ever you wish to…… for nada!

Marcus of !

www.plentyoffish

fame is the Sir Freddy laker of the chat world….ok lots of free sites are copying him!

The paying sites are changing their advertising.

75% off joining fee.

errrrrr for what..

what we can get for free.

Find love or guarantee your money back?

So?

We need to pay to find love?

Actually paying cash to a company will find love?

No!

What paying hard earned cash to a dating company …….will not find you love!

Mmmmm coffee just love that aroma.

Better than torre de muerde.

BULL SHIT!

Come on you paying sites!

YOU ARE COMING TO THE END OF YOUR LOLLIPOP!

SUCKS DOESN'T IT !

Actually shows in your advertising.

Now! Decide whom and whom not? you want to give your info to! If you go to the free sites!

Think about it!

No centrally stored data base?

Meaning? these companies can not sell, yes I said .sell your private information to?

Oh! you did not realize that the paying site companies did that!

Well they do!

How rude of them.

Invasive and

Totally the mistrust of these companies! getting your private information, gaining your trust at a great expense monetary from you. Then ! making, hm whoaa, more money from your Private information.

Naughty, naughty!

And not nice! People.

Dating Direct is sponsoring a television program? Nothing to do with romance. "Greys Anatomy"

A hospital? "A program about a hospital"

Ok a soap!

Dating Direct, now also advertising! oh on T.V.

Find romance?, or your money back?

The big fat fee you paid to join

No chance?

Read the small print.
You are probably paying to have." Greys Anatomy screened on tv"
Wakeup calls are probably in process from paying dating sites.
I see it in advertising from some potentially free sites?
Potentially free?
Plentymorefish.com

Chapter Fifteen

Cruising as a singleton on the many sites that are now out there!
Fa too many to mention?
I came across
www.plentymorefish.com
Is this Marcus Frind?
Marcus creating yet another site?The name is memorable?
Is it his site?
Or? A take on, on his original site?
Oh!
www.plentymoresilverfish.com
for the forty plus?
Ok so is it a free site just like Marcus's?
Hmmmmm
Actually free to join!
To make use of the I'm service you need to be a full member?
Once a full member you can enjoy all the features of
www.plentymoresilverfish.com

I just viewed the free ones on site? there were only a few tiddlers available!
So? If I want to see some big fish? I now have to pay.
1 month(30) days £9.99
oh nine ninety nine.
Oh wait a moment!
If I pay
3 months,(90) days! Do the fish get better?

6 months (180) days£29.99.

A whole year? (365) days, God gave us that for free!

Whoops, silly.

www.plentymoresilverfish

want you to pay £49.99 less than 14p per day To chat to the same person that you could have originally chatted to the same person? "heck .no.nerdthe free ones are the .What?

The expensive creative nice people start at

£9.99

Nine ninety nine! .whooo hoooooo.

Are they on sale?

Doahhhh! No

They are the exact same people that you can pay from nada to!

Trusting soles, these people signed up and gave all their information on joining!

The cost structure does not give out any more info that you originally gave from when you signed up initially!

Ok

The companies ..whom ever they may be?

You hook up with them! Ok!

We got that sussed?

We as trusting soles!, give them all the info they ask.

Name

d.o.b.

Tel: #

Mothers maiden name

Then

Some of these sites sell on our info to other dating sites with our photo.

From

£9.99, up to £49.99.

"So if you find a person you like the look of at lets say £9.99. Try to Chat and create a suitable dating fish line". Then! whoops before you realize that your conversation has run out and you become a £19.99Date!

to the same person? Just costs you more to chat to that very same person that originaly cost you

Nine ninety nine?

Talk and make arrangements quickly.

You could become?if you want to talk

Talk to the same person

@ £29.99.

Ok.

A free sign up?

With your already given details to the site are supposed to be classified information.

If you wish to know any more details about a possible beau, these are Classified as an upgrade which will cost you

£9,99 to £49.99

Sad,,,,,,,,,,,,

Fish food costs money? And lots of personal info from you.

Actually ..it is not possible to chat to ant one person free. You have to upgrade! For £££££. $$$$$ .. .

You have selected a feature only available to full members?

As a full member you can! Chat for

Nine ninety, nine! Supposedly!

Where is that god damn safety net from.

False advertising?

So……….

I am told that .

To use all the features of

www.plentymoresilverfish.com

I need to be a full member.

I can't even have a little fish?….err no……

I can see his photo…a little bio page………

But!

If!

I want to send a message it is going to cost me

£9.99

Nine ninety nine.

"I can guarantee. The site is using my bio page and photo to generate some male response". So.

"I joined the site. Gave my personal info very trustingly so". In the hope that the company would give my bio page and photo image. Get it out there to some guys? Apparently! not so? The information I gave to. .www.plentymoresilverfish.com

For free!.

They are now going to charge some men ££…$$ for my free info?..

CHAPTER SIXTEEN

Sort of sucks!

"So the dating scene has become a fish globe"?

.

Ok……….

The paying sites have to seriously clean up their acts!

Photo,s

Some of the photo's they allow to the profile do not match?

The bio page is ok. The photo is many years out of date!

I made arrangements to meet with some guys after plenty of conversation and cell phone calls! Arrange a suitable rendevous, On meeting usually a quick cell phone call to check out that each of us are close to the designated meeting point and voila something they ate or drank just put years on them…Like four to eight years…..Scary…..

Just makes you want to walk on water!

CHAPTER SEVENTEEN

James myself and the girls…plus our extended friends in story corner in Blues alley had decided enough was enough on our inter-net dating stories for today!

Tomorrow evening the girls myself and a few more friends of Jennies were meeting at the Mansion on O street for Dinner and a tour of the hotel which was also a museum quite a funky type of hotel! Ok some more chat about inter-net dating too. The general consensus was we had all had too many bad experiences and would just let things on the love scene happen cupid style!

We had all had enough of the

SCREW UP FAIRY!

The players the scammers and felons. These people are validating my inherent trust of strangers! Ok Internet fraud exists. The only safe way to avoid the baddies was to check them out via their IP addresses! This automatically compiles demographic information!

Retention of password confidentiality and user name is your sole responsibility.

The scary stuff is!

A computer …With a

IPS Provider

Along with an ims service…

CAN MAKE ME EMOTIONAL?

Look in the mirror? Slap yourself across the face! You may need to do this several times.

When you wake up?

The slap may have been harder than you wanted to do.

Depending on the amount of ims users you had contacted?

Ok!

Nerd?

There were more than you thought?

OK…….

Intensive care is not needed.

Alcohol is cool at this precise time and moment. I hold my hands up! I know the instant messaging is infectious so I decide to play tag before I go to meet the girls for dinner at the mansion!

www.tag.com is cool not invasive and you can have as much fun as you wish!….the ball is in your court.

A pleasant change from paying sites yet again!

I had arranged to meet Jan at her place of work on Connecticut avenue, downtown DC.

I was a little early so went to the basement of the building that she worked at. I had some time to kill so browsed the shops that were in the basement and decided to have a coffee!

There was a cute coffee bar located in the basement. Jan would be down to take the office post to the post office. "so we arranged to meet there when she finished work". The coffee bar had tables surrounding a water fountain so I chose a table next to the fountain!

Put my cell phone on the table and began to sip my skinny latte. "zoned out and began to day dream".

Excuse me mam? A boom mike was dropped in front of my face and a woman with a clipboard was navigating through the tables to reach my table next to the fountain?

I looked across to where the extended arm of the boom mike was being navigated from.

To my astonishment a camera was rolling and a news crew were asking me.

Mam! is that a Blackberry you have there on the table?

It was indeed a Blackberry! Normally I am quite virtuous. I removed the phone, before the woman reached my table. I became quite reticence! The guy with the boom mike was saying .Oh man I thought she had a Blackberry? Stop rolling. Phwww! Was I relieved.

CHAPTER EIGHTEEN

Back on the UK side of the pond I reflected on the stories about my friends and my own internet dating experiences!

In the relationship game! Timing is everything!. No matter how well you express yourself, things won't happen unless you tune into the desires of other people.

A constant challenge in relationships is to do and say the right things at the right time!

At this precise time and moment I would not make a good negotiator at a peace conference…

I need to change my outlook?

Most men I had dated were of a similar age to me!

Most men my age! Prefered, younger women!

It was usually accepted?

Get told this enough, it becomes a bit like the Stockholm syndrome?

For years it has been the norm for older men to chose a younger woman once he divorced his wife?

Times have changed? There has been a woman revolution!

Women are now a lot more independent!

Choosing careers, earning good salaries and divorcing their wayward husbands.

Women are getting divorce settlements, moving on and searching younger partners!

Physical age is the least defining characteristic?

Age does not always dictate maturity.

Step outside the box for insight to solutions logic sometimes can not handle!

Once upon a time!

I would never dream of dating a younger man!

I awoke from the dream!

www.lulu.com/paulinesmart

www.ingramcontent.com/pod-product-compliance
Ingram Content Group UK Ltd.
Pitfield, Milton Keynes, MK11 3LW, UK
UKHW041925190726
13854UKWH00003B/1450

9 780557 001460